A DEFENCE OF
THEOLOGICAL ETHICS

A DEFENCE OF
THEOLOGICAL ETHICS

HULSEAN LECTURES 1964

BY

G. F. WOODS, B.D.

Professor of Divinity in the University of London
Honorary Fellow of Downing College, Cambridge

CAMBRIDGE
AT THE UNIVERSITY PRESS
1966

PUBLISHED BY

THE SYNDICS OF THE CAMBRIDGE UNIVERSITY PRESS

Bentley House, 200 Euston Road, London, N.W.1

American Branch: 32 East 57th Street, New York, N.Y. 10022

West African Office: P.M.B. 5181, Ibadan, Nigeria

©

CAMBRIDGE UNIVERSITY PRESS

1966

Printed in Great Britain at the University Printing House, Cambridge
(Brooke Crutchley, University Printer)

LIBRARY OF CONGRESS CATALOGUE

CARD NUMBER: 66–11032

PREFACE

The Editor of *Soundings* wrote, 'The authors of this volume of essays cannot persuade themselves that the time is ripe for major works of theological construction or reconstruction. It is a time for ploughing, not reaping; or, to use the metaphor we have chosen for our title, it is a time for making soundings, not charts or maps.'[1] I believe that the same is true in the realm of christian ethical theory. No one who understands the gravity and complexity of the present situation can expect quick and simple answers to the problems which press upon us. In this course of Hulsean Lectures, I have given a limited study to a limited theme. My main concern has been the moral challenge to christian theological ethics from the secular humanist who has a high sense of moral responsibility without any belief in God or in personal immortality. I have not had primarily in mind those who have adopted complete moral relativism or scepticism. Nor have I been thinking of those who have lapsed into chronic cynicism. My aim has been to show that those who are in agreement in accepting a genuine moral standard and the duty of responsible conduct may profitably consider whether these may be more reasonably and adequately understood in terms of secular humanism or christian theism. It is my opinion that christian theological ethics do justice to what is true in the ethics of responsible secular humanism and deal with a number of fundamental questions arising from

[1] *Soundings*, ed. A. R. Vidler (1962), p. ix.

our moral experience to which the secular humanist does not always give sufficient attention.

As I am convinced that our understanding of the more mysterious features of the world of our experience is deeply influenced by the words we use, I have found it necessary to spend considerable time analysing the variety of ways in which we speak of the nature, expression and application of what we call standards. In our present situation, I do not think that this time has been wasted. We have to learn to look through the words we use if they are to be useful to us in illuminating what is obscure. This is specially important when we are using words analogically.

I realise that these lectures only touch upon the ultimate questions about the nature and status of moral personal being, but I hope that they may enable some secular humanists and some christians to enter upon conversations which may prove useful to both.

G. F. W.

King's College London
April 1965

CONTENTS

LECTURE 1

CHALLENGES TO
THEOLOGICAL ETHICS

These lectures will consider the contemporary challenge from the type of secular humanism which accepts a high moral standard without professing any belief in God or in personal survival after death.

This challenge combines metaphysical and moral criticisms of theological ethics.

The moral criticisms are made upon the basis of belief in the autonomy of ethics. This is the belief that the autonomous moral standard requires no theological foundation and that the autonomous moral agent is not morally justified in seeking or accepting divine assistance.

In order to clarify the points in dispute between the secular humanist and the christian, it is necessary to examine the vocabulary which both are using in speaking of the moral standard.

The claim is made that an analysis of physical and personal standards and a study of the various ways in which the autonomy of ethics may be interpreted will make it less difficult to advance towards an interpretation of the moral standard as the creative and saving will of God, as these are understood in liberal christian theology.

CHALLENGES TO
THEOLOGICAL ETHICS

The Hulsean Lectures are based upon a generous benefaction made to the University of Cambridge in the late eighteenth century by the Reverend John Hulse. He was born in Cheshire in 1708 and in 1724 he entered St John's College. In his will he made a variety of provisions for the advancement and reward of religious learning. The main purpose of these was to defend the 'Truth and Excellency of Christianity'. It seems, therefore, not inappropriate that in this course of lectures I should offer some defence of the Truth and Excellency of Christian Theological Ethics. The title, I admit, sounds slightly provocative and may raise hopes which I know I am quite unable to fulfil but I will try to speak as simply and clearly as I can upon a theme which is, I believe, a grave issue for those of us who accept the christian tradition and a matter of genuine interest to many who now no longer feel able to accept the christian faith.

In this introductory lecture, I have three major aims in view. In the first place, I wish to review and identify the main contemporary challenges to christian theological ethics. As in a short course of lectures it would have been too cumbersome to give an adequate account of a whole series of objections raised by individual writers,[1] I have

[1] Cf. W. G. Maclagan, *The Theological Frontier of Ethics* (1961); R. W. Hepburn, *Christianity and Paradox* (1958); G. E. Moore, *Principia Ethica* (1903).

tried instead to classify the main objections which are being made. My second aim is to select the challenges which I take to be most serious at the present time and most appropriate for immediate consideration. My third aim is to give some indication of the general course of the later lectures, without, of course, anticipating the detailed argument of each lecture.

The verb 'to challenge' originally meant 'to accuse falsely', but it would clearly be prejudging the issue to assume that this is the true nature of all the challenges to theological ethics. The whole point is whether these challenges are true or false. We cannot settle this issue by discussing challenges in general. Each challenge requires individual study. In battle the danger is not from gunfire in general but from the particular shell which explodes near the place where you happen to be at the time. Each actual challenge takes place in a particular historical situation. It is an historical event. It participates, therefore, in all the relativities and particularities of human history. It shares many of the characteristics of the age in which it is made. Both the challenge which is offered and the conception of theological ethics at which the challenge is directed are involved in the whole confused course of human history. And no challenge is ever a wholly contemporary matter. The past remains influential in the present. This influence is both recognised and unrecognised. We may be open to the future but our thinking and our speech are largely shaped by the multitude of our known and unknown predecessors. We play our contemporary parts in the philosophical disputation but we have not invented the words which we use or the structure of the conceptual building in which the disputation is held. These considerations might suggest that our study of the challenges to theological ethics ought to have been fundamentally historical. I believe that this would have been illuminating. I am sure that all philosophical thinking about human personality is deepened and enriched by a wide knowledge of human history and a sound historical judgement. We cannot expect to understand the historical changes in the uses of words if we know nothing of the historical situations in which they have been used.[1]

But such vast undertakings are beyond the scope of the present lectures. I have chosen the less ambitious course of beginning with the identification of the various types of challenges which are being made in the contemporary situation. I think that a broad distinction may be drawn between those which are primarily metaphysical and those which are primarily moral. I say primarily metaphysical and primarily moral because at this stage I am making no more than a working distinction for the sake of clarity in exposition.

It is obvious that the major metaphysical challenge to theological ethics is an explicit denial of the existence of God. Those who have no belief in natural or revealed theology can have no place for a theological interpretation of ethics. But these explicit denials are lacking in definite meaning until more is known of the concept of God which is being denied and the type of denial which is being made. Atheism is meaningless if theism is not given a reasonably clear meaning. Obviously, the type of metaphysical objection to christian theological ethics which is most serious

[1] Cf. D. M. MacKinnon, *A Study in Ethical Theory* (1957).

is the denial of God as understood in the christian tradition. Even this more precisely defined denial may take many forms. There may be a total rejection of the christian tradition about God or more limited denials or misgivings about some traditional feature or attribute of the christian conception of God. Many critics, for example, have deep misgivings about the philosophical propriety of thinking of God in personal terms. This anxiety is naturally deepest where no justification is seen for the use of analogy in thinking and speaking about God. Another series of objections springs from metaphysical beliefs about the existence and nature of human personality. Where it is thought that personal being may be completely explained away in terms which are impersonal, no place is left for the ordinary interpretation of moral action as the activity of a free moral agent. The precise manner in which individual personality is explained away is immaterial. The existence of personal being is denied when it is no longer believed that persons ultimately transcend their circumstances. I suspect that for many of my contemporaries belief in the existence of the soul is a more significant issue than the existence of God. Any belief that an individual human being is no more than the transitory intersection of a variety of causal series is plainly incompatible with the tradition of christian ethics in which the hope of eternal life has always been an essential element.

It would be tedious (if, indeed, it has not already become so) to give a more extended list of the metaphysical challenges, but my present concern is with the challenges which are primarily moral. I still believe that in the end the metaphysical issues are supreme, but progress at this point is delayed because there is at the moment no general agreement about the meaning, the possibility or the methods of metaphysics. The moral challenges are more clearly articulated and there is a good reason why christians should consider these seriously. This reason is that in any defence of christian ethics, or of any alternative type of ethics, appeal must finally be made to the moral experience of those who are engaged in the debate and to the wider moral experience of thoughtful and responsible people who have a deep and varied acquaintance with human life. Moral issues can only be considered within the context of moral experience. It follows that any moral challenge to the christian ethical position is more than an external challenge of a wholly alien character. The serious defender and the serious critic of the christian ethical tradition are both appealing to moral insight and each must respect the moral integrity of his opponent. The conflicts which arise often lack, therefore, the crude simplicity of the battles which follow a formal declaration of war between two wholly separate nations. The situation has something of the frustration and even tragedy of a civil war in which both contestants may honestly believe that they are serving the true interests of their country.

As my hope in these lectures is not to increase but to diminish the confusions of the present conflicts about christian ethics, I must select and describe the moral challenge which I consider to be most serious in the present day. I will call it secular humanism. No short title is ever either quite plain or quite fair. I must explain more precisely what I take it to mean. In saying that this humanism is secular, I am assuming that it includes either an explicit denial of the existence of God or a kind of verbal assent without any very conscious reference to God when serious moral decisions are being made. I also assume it includes an explicit denial of any individual life after death or a belief in some sort of immortality which is so vague as to be customarily neglected in any discussion of a substantial moral problem. Here, I must emphasise that I am not judging but simply describing what I take to be the main negative characteristics of secular humanism. These are more easily defined than its more positive characteristics. I am not here concerning myself with types of humanism which appear to be entirely sceptical about the reality of moral standards or wholly cynical about the ability of human beings to live in accord with the moral standards which they profess. The secular humanism which I have in mind is characterised by a high sense of moral responsibility in both private and public life.

This kind of secular humanism has one characteristic conviction which seems to be the basis of a whole series of moral criticisms of theological ethics. This is a belief in the autonomy of ethics. In a later lecture I shall be examining this phrase in greater detail but it is usually a combination of belief in the autonomy of the moral standard and belief in the autonomy of the moral agent. Each is taken to be in some sense free from some kind of moral subordination to something other than itself. Both the moral standard and the moral agent are believed to possess some kind of irreducible moral independence. It is plain that this belief in the autonomy of ethics may lead to a series of moral objections to christian theological ethics. I will remind you, in the first place, of objections which are based upon belief in the autonomy of the moral standard and then mention those which derive from belief in the autonomy of the moral agent.

The humanist who believes in the autonomy of the moral standard naturally finds great difficulty in seeing the moral relevance of the major christian doctrines. He accepts the moral standard for its own sake. For him it stands in its own right. Though we all meet many difficult moral problems, in most cases our duty is quite plain. Simple acts of kindness and compassion appear to be morally admirable in themselves without any reference to divine support or approval. On many morally common-place occasions, there seems to be no moral necessity to make any mention of God or to refer to the hope of eternal life. Wanton cruelty, it is said, can be seen to be wrong without any remoter justification. And, in more complex cases, where moral deliberation is required, it is often difficult to see how the final moral considerations are morally related to the articles of the christian faith. The christian doctrines seem to be morally irrelevant whether they are true or not. Other secular humanists have a more positive and militant attitude towards theological ethics. They may find that any reference to a theological basis of morality is offensive to them. Their contention is that the autonomous moral standard not only needs no support from God but that it would be immoral for the moral stan-dard to have moral support. It is said, for example, that to interpret the moral standard as the will of God is bound to lead to insoluble moral problems. We must try to ap-preciate how these problems arise. The first point is that an appeal to ordinary moral experience shows that a human will is not a good will solely in view of the fact that it is the actual will of a human being. For example, an order issued by a military officer is not morally good or bad solely in view of the fact that the order has been issued. The fact that an order is given does not settle the issue whether it is morally right or wrong. It might be either. The second point is that we run into great moral difficulties in understanding the moral standard as the will of God if we think of the divine will as very similar to the human will. We may think that what is good is what God wills or that God wills the good because he sees that it is good. On the first alternative, the impression is given that the moral standard is the outcome of the arbitrary will of God. He might have willed lying to be a virtue. On the other alternative, we are moving towards the admission that God himself is subordinate to a moral standard which he recognises but does not create. In one case the moral quality of the moral standard appears to be lost, and in the other God seems to have no part in establishing or maintaining the moral standard. The essence of the challenge is that a wholly autonomous standard requires no divine support and is morally degraded when it is given.

Somewhat similar moral puzzles are found in the efforts to understand how belief in individual immortality is morally relevant to belief in an autonomous moral standard. If it is plainly right that I ought to be helpful to my neighbour, in what way does belief in his immortality and my own morally affect my duty towards him? Would disbelief in immortality really make me take a different view of my plain duty? And am I not in the moral danger of thinking that I ought to do my duty in order to obtain everlasting life? Is there not a moral risk that I may be using other people as a means for gaining my own salvation? Am I, as has been said, using other people as a kind of silver polish to burnish ever more brilliantly the fine metal of my own character? Would it not be morally simpler to accept the moral standard for its own sake and to leave aside the question of belief in survival after death? The present point at issue in these and similar puzzles is not whether belief in individual immortality is true but whether this belief has or ought to have any moral relevance to the moral standard, and, if so, in what way.

Another way of expressing essentially the same kind of problem about the relation of the moral standard to the will of God is the familiar theme of the distinction between judging what is the case and judging what ought to be the case. These appear to be two logically distinct kinds of judgement which are not deducible one from the other. If I say that it is the case that someone has failed to repay a debt, I am stating that in fact the debt has not been repaid. I am not saying that the debt ought to have been repaid. This further judgement may be morally justified but it is not included in the factual judgement that no repayment has been made. It is a moral, not a descriptive, judgement. Similarly, there is no logical step from the judgement that the debt ought to have been repaid to the judgement that in fact it has been repaid. Many business people must regret that this is not so. The relevance of this logical problem to many issues in the field of theological ethics is obvious. Can we, for example, logically move from an affirmation of the existence of God to an affirmation that God is morally good? If we cannot do so, how are we to

understand the relation of the existence and the goodness
of God? Are we bound to think of each of these in isolation from the other? And how are we to think of the
relation of God to the moral standard? If we believe that
the moral standard expresses the will of God, how can we
advance to the affirmation that the standard which he wills
is morally good? This kind of problem, to which I know
of no quick and simple answer, represents in a logical form
the basic problem of reconciling the autonomy of the
moral standard with an acceptance of theological ethics.

The moral challenges which we have so far noticed
have been based upon the secular humanist's view of the
nature and status of the moral standard considered in
itself. There is another class of critical comments which
are directed not so much against the theological understanding of the moral standard as against various expressions and applications of the christian moral tradition.
These are adversely criticised by reference to a moral
standard to which the christian moral tradition is expected
to conform. The point of attack is not the moral status of
the christian standard in itself but some of the ways in
which the standard has been formulated and applied.
There is, for example, the charge that morally unfortunate
endeavours have been made to express the christian standard in terms of absolute rules to which there can be no
exceptions. This is said to be incompatible with a morally
sensitive interpretation of moral laws as general directives
which may rightly be adapted to special circumstances.
The whole contemporary interest in situational and con-
textual ethics is hostile to any absolute expressions or
absolute applications of a moral standard and, conse-

quently, to any interpretation of the christian standard in this way.

It is an accident of history that this challenge to theological ethics as legalistic has taken the particular form of moral criticism of absolute moral laws to which no exceptions are allowed. In other ages, the criticism has been that theological morality was a vast code of detailed precepts and rules which purported to cover every conceivable case. It was then possible to say that such detailed guidance impeded the growth of the moral agent towards moral maturity. He remained in infantile subjection to a vast number of detailed regulations. It could also be objected that these codes of conduct led to endless and fruitless debates about the application of a particular regulation to a particular case and that there was no way of meeting unprecedented moral problems. Basically, the moral objection is the same whether it is directed against a few allegedly absolute rules or against a multitude of detailed regulations. In either case, there is a moral objection against any acceptance of these formulations as true expressions of the autonomous moral standard. There is a general impression that theological ethics are morally inadequate in that they are incapable of responding to exceptional situations and take no effective account of the rapid advance in many fields of modern knowledge.

There are also quite a number of more detailed criticisms of particular traditional formulations of the christian moral standard, for example, about the indissolubility of marriage. These particular moral issues, which are of genuine moral concern to both christians and secularists, require constant and careful study but I do not propose in this course of lectures to examine in detail any of these outstanding moral problems. My concern is with a general defence of christian theological ethics and in the last few minutes I have been outlining some of the primarily moral objections which are made to theological ethics upon the basis of the autonomy of the moral standard. Each was a variation upon the same theme. The first form of the objection was that an autonomous moral standard required no theological basis though there was no moral objection to the holding of the christian faith by those who found it credible. As theological convictions were irrelevant to the authority of the autonomous moral standard, individuals could be left to profess whatever theological beliefs they found useful. This first form of objection could be more explicitly hostile to theological ethics on the ground that the autonomy of the moral standard would inevitably be degraded if it were subordinated to some authority other than its own. There were definite moral objections to theological ethics as such. The second form of the objection was that there was no logically permissible transition from judgements about what is the case to judgements about what ought to be the case, and that, in consequence, statements about the existence of God and about a future life had no clear moral relevance to the autonomy of the moral standard. The third form of the objection was not so much against the nature of the theological moral standard in itself as against the danger of formalism and legalism in its expression and application. Finally, there was a series of more particular moral objections based upon an autonomous moral standard against various features of traditional christian morality.

Though a great deal more ought to be said about all these objections, I must now turn to those which spring from a belief in the autonomy of the moral agent. The debate about freewill and determinism is interminable or, at least, it has not yet terminated. No conclusion to the debate is in sight. It has been said, rather pessimistically, that all arguments lead to determinism and all experience leads to belief in freewill. However that may be, I believe I am right in thinking that the secular humanists who have a high sense of moral responsibility, both individual and corporate, continue to believe in the moral freedom of the moral agent. They generally hold that people are usually morally responsible for what they do and what they do not do. Admittedly, the contemporary world is far less certain than earlier generations about the exact degree of moral responsibility in particular cases. Much more is known and accepted about the factors, both physical and psychological, which diminish the degree of responsibility. But I think that those who continue to accept the autonomy of the moral standard tend also to accept the autonomy of the moral agent. They usually affirm that to have a sense of being under an obligation to the moral law implies an ability on our part to will to fulfil it. Circumstances may prevent the outward actions to which we feel obliged but we are free to obey or to disobey in our intentions. And our attention is drawn to the common experience of serious remorse and guilt. Their general view of the moral agent is that he is autonomous in the sense that his decisions and actions have grounds and not merely causes. He is morally more than a leaf carried along by the stream of events. He acts on some understanding of the moral standard and upon his knowledge of the facts of the moral case in which he must act. In some sense his activity is genuinely and inescapably his own, however much he may later wish to dissociate himself from what he did or failed to do. Man is taken to be at once a genuine agent and a genuinely moral agent.

This robust belief in the autonomy of the moral agent is the source of a group of moral problems about the place of grace in christian ethics. This is the perpetual dispute about faith and works. The essence of the problem is to understand how any man can at one and the same time remain an autonomous moral agent and receive the assistance of divine grace. The two seem to be irreconcilable. It is by no means difficult to see how this series of objections arises and we ought to study them fairly and carefully. A confident believer in the ability and freedom of a normal moral agent to do either what is right or what is wrong may quite honestly claim that he can see no need for divine grace. In his view, the ordinary man needs no divine help in the business of acting morally. He is simply free to do good or to do evil. A morally mature person will be conscious of no need for divine help. Speaking rather more carefully, this is not a moral objection to the possibility of divine aid but a simple statement that a mature moral agent has no need for it. The primarily moral misgivings arise about the propriety of either receiving or giving divine grace. If the moral worth of an action depends upon the moral freedom of the agent, it is morally difficult to see how anyone can be entitled to help him or in what way he may be entitled to receive help. Both operations appear to be morally indefensible. It looks like a case of a schoolmaster surreptitiously giving help to one of his pupils who is sitting a public examination. It is morally wrong both to give and to accept the assistance in the circumstances. His activity then appears manifestly unjust. If, therefore, the operation of grace is understood in similar terms, it must appear to be open to many moral objections by those who believe that there is a moral standard by reference to which the acts of God may be judged.

Christians have not been unaware of these moral problems about divine grace but they are bound to claim that grace is of the essence of the christian gospel. This is more than the result of the historical fact that the idea of divine grace is so interwoven into the texture of the New Testament that it cannot be removed without tearing the fabric of the text. It does not just happen to be a fact in the historical tradition. The christian has moral grounds for claiming that without grace there is no gospel. It is taken to be an essential characteristic of the saving will of God that he is willing to save even those who do not strictly merit salvation. To the christian it is morally intolerable that salvation is offered only to those who deserve it. On that basis we have no hope. The gospel is good news precisely because it offers hope to those who have lost all hope of being entitled to salvation. It is more than a conditional offer of help to those who can fulfil the necessary conditions. But it must be candidly admitted that a refusal to abandon belief in the operation of the grace of God is no answer to the serious moral problems which arise when an effort is made to reconcile the operation of grace with the autonomy of the moral agent.

Having given some account of the contemporary form

of some of the traditional challenges to christian theological ethics, I now wish to explain to you in outline the course of the later lectures and to give some of the reasons that have led me to select the course which I have chosen. I have given a report of some of the primarily metaphysical and the primarily moral objections to christian theological ethics and I have said that my main concern is with the general outlook represented by the type of secular humanism which has a profound respect for the moral standard and a deep sense of moral responsibility. I explained that I had in mind those who have a genuine regard for the moral law and a deep sense of duty combined with an explicit or virtual disbelief in the major christian doctrines and a series of sincere moral objections to theological ethics, and more particularly to christian theological ethics. I believe that, in listening to the challenges which are being made, many of us will have felt that the conflict is one in which our moral sympathies oscillate between one side and the other. I find myself that I have sympathy with both sides. The points of dispute appear to be clear at one moment and lacking all clarity at the next. The fog of war has not lifted.

We cannot hope for a clear solution to a problem which remains obscurely understood. As we do most of our thinking and discussing in words, it is essential that we should take care in the way in which we use them. Most of our words are very overburdened beasts of burden. This is true of the words used in the discussion of metaphysical and moral problems. We must perpetually be scrutinising both our verbal and conceptual apparatus and the matter itself about which we are trying to think and to speak. I am proposing, therefore, to spend the next two lectures in a consideration of the ways in which we use the word 'standard' when we are speaking of physical and personal standards. These will prepare the way for an examination of the use of the phrase 'the autonomy of ethics', which I am taking to include belief both in an autonomous moral standard and in the autonomy of the moral agent. I shall then be able in the concluding lectures to look at christian theological ethics, making the somewhat artificial distinction between the creative and the saving will of God. I hope to commend to you the view that in christian theological ethics we have an interpretation of our moral experience which does justice to what is true in secular humanist ethics and offers some answers to a number of problems to which I do not think the secular humanist gives sufficient attention.

I am bound to confess that those who are acquainted with the terms of the will of the Reverend John Hulse may justifiably feel that the type of defence of christian theological ethics which I am proposing lamentably fails to fulfil the somewhat exacting description that he gives of the proper duties of the Christian Advocate or the Hulsean Lecturer. It is, he says, the duty of the Lecturer to 'shew the evidence for Revealed Religion, and to demonstrate in the most convincing and persuasive manner the Truth and Excellency of Christianity... or any particular article or branch thereof, and chiefly against notorious infidels, whether atheists or deists, not descending to any particular sects or controversies (so much to be lamented) amongst Christians themselves'. This pleasantly rational and unsectarian approach, is somewhat abandoned in the next sentence, which continues, 'Except some new or dangerous error of superstition or enthusiasm, as of Popery or Methodism or the like, either in opinion or practice shall prevail, in which case only, it may be necessary for that time to write and preach against the same.'

I certainly have no intention of lecturing against Popery or Methodism but I earnestly hope to avoid the detestable alternatives of superstition on the one hand and enthusiasm on the other.

LECTURE 2

PHYSICAL STANDARDS

As we have a natural tendency to think of the moral standard in terms drawn from our experience of physical standards, it is necessary to inquire how these are established, expressed and applied.

A study of the medieval Royal Standard Yard preserved in a Winchester museum discloses some of the characteristics of an official physical standard of length.

Other physical standards have an even greater variety in their modes of establishment, expression and application.

All physical standards have the curious character of not being identical with their expressions and applications, while being in some way authoritatively related to both. This relationship is bound to be misunderstood if we think of the standard itself in physical terms. There are no physical standards.

PHYSICAL STANDARDS

In my previous lecture I was speaking of the contemporary challenges to theological ethics and of the course which I intended to follow in the rest of these lectures. I suggested that the contemporary forms of the traditional challenges to christian theological ethics might be distinguished into those which were primarily metaphysical and those which were primarily moral. I did not wish to imply that this working distinction was either clear or absolute. I explained that I intended to give my main attention to the moral challenges because the state of metaphysics at the moment was too fluid to allow of any assured acts of reconstruction and because those still standing in the christian tradition were most sensitive to the challenges and criticisms which appeared to have a plain moral basis. I compared the tension which arose between the christians and their critics as comparable to the confused hostilities of a civil war in which the contestants often found the loyalties of their own hearts divided. When both parties appealed sincerely to moral insight, it was not possible to dismiss what was said as morally irresponsible. I said, therefore, that in my opinion the most serious contemporary challenge to christian ethics came from those who rejected theological ethics on moral grounds. This general attitude was typical of what I called secular humanism. This was secular in its explicit or virtual denial of the christian faith and it was humanist in the sense of having a high regard for the dignity of human nature. A central conviction of this type of secular humanism was a firm belief in the autonomy of ethics. This usually combined a belief in the autonomy of the moral standard with a belief in the autonomy of the moral agent. From this basic conviction sprang a number of moral objections to theological ethics. It could appear that the major christian doctrines were morally irrelevant to the authority of the moral standard. A sharper criticism was that on moral grounds it was offensive to offer or to accept a theological basis for the autonomous moral standard and that the operation of divine grace without regard to merit was contrary to natural justice. There were also a number of moral objections to christian theological ethics as unduly legalistic and unresponsive to the moral demands of special situations. This was a particularly serious defect in any moral standard for the present age of rapid advance in our knowledge of the natural world and of the inner workings of the human soul. Finally, on the basis of an independent and autonomous moral standard, a number of criticisms were made of the traditional christian attitude on such particular moral issues as the indissolubility of marriage.

As both christians and secular humanists of the kind which I have in mind are agreed in the respect which they have for the moral standard, it seems to me to be essential to examine carefully our use of the word 'standard'. Misunderstanding and misuse of this key word may easily cloud and distort the issues which require attention. I am therefore devoting the present lecture to a study of physical standards and the next lecture to a study of personal standards. I believe that in so doing I shall be freeing my mind from a number of prejudices with which I may otherwise approach a reconsideration of christian theological ethics. A deeper understanding of the uses of the word in the fields of physical and personal standardisation may release me from a series of mistaken expectations about the ways in which the moral standard is established, expressed and applied. Though I believe that a clearer understanding of the use of the word in other fields may later assist me in appreciating its appropriateness and its inappropriateness in the realm of morality, I do not wish to confine my present examination of physical and personal standards simply to what may prove to be useful later. If I am too concerned to notice the future utility of any observation which I now make, I shall give the impression that, like an experienced conjuror, I am deftly placing the rabbit in the hat before the performance in order to prepare for the moment of feigned surprise when it duly appears later in the programme.

Before entering upon a study of a particular physical standard, I must give some account of my understanding of the way we use words in the interpretation of our experience. In practice it seems impossible to divide our experience and our interpretation of our world. We find that what we take to be our simplest experiences involves some kind of interpretation of the constitution and course of the world. The act of experiencing is an act of interpretation. I do not believe that what we can experience is limited to what we can put clearly into words. There are moments of profound human experience in which we are at a loss for words or feel that the experience might be lost if we tried to put it into words. It is an occupational weakness of members of the scholastic profession to assume that the only purpose of silence is to provide an opportunity for something to be said either by others or, more usually, by themselves. Silence is not always a sign of stupidity. Even so, there is undoubtedly a strong inclination to express our experiences verbally. In a sense, we often possess them more fully when they are appropriately formulated in words. And, certainly, we value words as one of the least inadequate means of communication. We have a natural desire to share many of our experiences with others who are capable of the same kind of experience. The origin of the words which we employ is usually quite unknown but on many occasions it is plain that we are extending the use of a word by transferring it from the site in which it has traditionally been used. We have found the word useful in a commonplace situation and we transfer it for use in a novel situation. We use the word analogically. This use of analogy is very widespread in our everyday language and is far more than the employment of two words where one would do. The justification of its use is that we are speaking of something which is less well known in terms of something which is better known. For example, when I spoke a moment ago of 'transferring' a word from one site to another, I was speaking analogically. 'To transfer' is 'to carry across'. Because we all have experience of carrying things, we can in a sense understand what is meant when people speak of 'transferring' a word from one place to another. To think and speak of what takes place as a 'transference' is in some ways illuminating and in other ways misleading. The carrying of a burden and the transference of a word are not two ways of describing exactly the same operation. This is the fascination and the difficulty about all analogies. They are neither wholly appropriate nor wholly inappropriate. They can work well but never perfectly. Their reputation waxes and wanes. They are always open both to praise and to blame. In some ways they are most dangerous when they are most successful. A highly appropriate analogy may induce a habit of philosophical inattention which may prevent us observing the point or points at which the analogy is misleading. I suspect that this may often happen when we are thinking or speaking of the moral standard as a standard.

If this account of the use of words in the interpretation of our experience is not wholly inaccurate, we can see many ways in which I may fall into error in my use of words. Though many of these errors may be essentially verbal, it is an error to assert that they are all linguistic. I may be so fundamentally mistaken about the interpretation of some situation in which I find myself that it is misleading to say that the misapprehension is purely a matter of language. For example, an anglican bishop, who was due to preach at Downing College a few years ago, was to have come from the station in a taxi but it happened that he was enthusiastically met by a representative of one of the Free Churches who had been deputed to meet a bishop and the mistake in identification was not discovered until far up Hills Road the bishop ventured to mention that he thought Downing College was in the other direction. This sheer mistake was no doubt in some measure a mistake in spoken and unspoken words but the heart of the matter was a sheer mistake about what was the case. But the fact that some basic mistakes are about the facts must not blind us to the fact that many philosophical mistakes and puzzles are due to mistakes in the use of words. These may occur at a number of stages. We may be initially misled by failing to detect the inadequacies in the analogical uses of words which have become so commonplace that we have forgotten that they are being used analogically. It might be claimed that in these cases we really know their limitations and their tendency to distort our vision. I am not at all convinced that this is so. I believe that this largely unconscious analogical use of words disposes us to think of what is before us in terms of the earlier situation in which the word had its primary use. We are, moreover, unconsciously inclined to think not simply in terms of the local situation in which the word was originally at home but in terms of the view of the world in which the local situation was possible. Each word which is used analogically tends to suggest the abiding presence of the world view held by those who originally used it. For example, I think we shall find that even in speaking about physical standards we are often using forgotten analogies. In recognising their analogical character we need not conclude that they are useless but we may be prompted to look more clearly at what actually occurs when physical standards are established and used. The second stage at which serious errors may happen is when we transfer without due care and attention the whole vocabulary of physical or personal standards for use in our thinking and speaking about the moral standard. This may seem an obvious, but it may prove an unfortunate, procedure. Second-hand words, like second-hand clothes, may happen to fit reasonably well, but we cannot assume that they will always do so. I suggest, therefore, that in thinking about physical standards we must not assume that there are no sheer mistakes in our present thinking and we must be on our guard against a slipshod use of the traditional terminology about them. Above all, we must not assume that in gaining a better understanding of physical standards we are automatically gaining a more sensitive insight into the nature and operation of the moral standard.

I begin my examination of the uses of the word 'standard' by making the blatantly obvious remark that a standard is originally something which stands. The word suggests a pillar or post which stands upright. Initially, there may have been a suggestion that, as men can only remain standing by intending to do so, even pillars and posts would have fallen to the ground if they had not had some intention of remaining upright. When the word was used to refer to a flagpole, it was in some ways a natural transition to apply it to the flag which was flown. In the military use of the word, it referred to the standard of the general on the field of battle. Prior to communication by radio and telephone, it was convenient to be able to identify the headquarters to which information could be sent and from which military orders could be issued. This line of development leads towards the description of the flag which signifies the personal presence of the sovereign as the Royal Standard.

This discontinuity between the use of the word in reference to flags and its use in reference to the moral standard is so great that it is obviously more profitable to turn at once to a study of the medieval use of the word in reference to physical standards of weight and measure. Let us take a simple illustration which will prove to be less simple than it looks. In the West Gate museum at Winchester there is a fine display of medieval standard weights and measures. Many of these were the royal standards of the time. One of these is the Royal Standard Yard. This is a beautifully made metal bar which is stamped with the Royal Arms. Presumably, this was kept in official custody and duly applied in cases of public dispute about the accuracy of some measurement. It was the standard to which the king's subjects could appeal. It must have been final in the sense that no one could challenge the royal standard by reference to some private standard of his own. The king's standard possessed sovereignty. It was subject to no other.

Now I think we may make a number of serious mistakes in our understanding of this apparently simple case of a physical standard. In the first place, we may identify the royal standard with the metal bar. This is an error. The bar itself is simply the bar which it is. It has no obligation to be longer or shorter than it is and no other bar or measurable object has any obligation to be the same length as the bar. The actual bar is no more than a physical expression or exemplar of the unit of length which at the material time is called a yard. The manufactured bar is the outcome of a number of decisions. There was the royal decision that the yard should be one of the national units of length and there was the consequent decision to have a bar made which should be the duly authenticated replica or representation of this standard unit of length. The bar is not the standard. The standard itself is elusive. It is not identical with any of its physical expressions but it is somehow represented in them. This means that we are not speaking carefully in referring to physical standards because no standard is in itself physical. It is intimately related to its physical expression but it is not the same thing. This misunderstanding even of a comparatively simple physical standard should make us cautious in assuming that we have a sufficiently clear appreciation of our use of the word 'standard' in regard to physical standards to justify us in using the word as a useful analogy in talking about the moral standard. We may make the mistake of thinking that we can adequately understand the moral standard in terms of our misunderstanding of physical standards.

In the second place, we may make the mistake of assuming that because the number of inches in a yard might have been different, the final choice of thirty-six was purely arbitrary. This is not so. An arbitrary decision is not necessarily a capricious one. We do not suppose that the decisions of a court of arbitration are arbitrary in the sense that they are not based on good reasons. To become a total abstainer is in a sense an arbitrary decision but we do not usually assume that total abstainers are irresponsible. The decision to establish the yard as a public unit of length was based upon a number of obvious and reasonable considerations. It was a convenient unit of length which suited the broad needs of the market-place and the battlefield. Moreover, it was appropriate in relation to the normal size and shape of the human body. If men were sixteen feet high and all their limbs were of a proportionate length, I suppose that our public units of length would have been very different. We know quite well that traditional units of length may be modified later in the light of new needs and changing circumstances. These modifications are not arbitrary in the sense of being pointless. The arbitrariness in the physical expression of physical standards is also not irrational. There were good practical reasons for representing the royal yard by a metal bar. It remained virtually the same length in all foreseeable circumstances. It was easily portable from place to place. It occupied very little storage space. It was durable. Being in the form of a bar it was conveniently shaped for use on most, though not all, occasions. It was, for example, not a convenient instrument for measuring the circumference of a standing tree. Had the art of manufacturing metal instruments been more highly developed at the time, we might have had a series of royal standard metal tape measures. In short, though there was freedom of choice in choosing the physical form of a bar, it was not an accidental or capricious choice. It was a deliberately chosen expression. There was a similar absence of thoughtless arbitrariness in the application of the standard bar. It was applied in accordance with an agreed procedure. It was, for instance, not placed diagonally across a piece of cloth which was to be measured. The whole operation was influenced by a series of quite reasonable and quite definite conventions. Many of them were so obvious that there was no need to have an official description of what was to be done. By the common consent of the contending parties, of the officials who were present, and of the general public the act of applying the bar would take place in the ordinary manner. Without these implicit and explicit agreements about its use, the bar would have been useless as a physical expression of the Royal Standard Yard. It would have been as useless as the instruments for playing a game without any instructions about the rules of the game. This curious combination of freedom and lack of freedom in making arbitrary decisions about the establishment, expression and application of physical standards is liable to prejudice our thinking later about the senses in which the moral standard may be legitimately described as arbitrary. We ought always to try to avoid in the field of philosophical ethics the danger comparable to the error in the military field of fighting a new war with the mentality and weapons of an earlier one.

We might, in passing, notice that we may learn further lessons about the operation of applying standards by marking the occasions on which we know that it is impracticable to apply them. For example, no one ever thought that it would be practicable to measure the distance from the earth to the sun by the diligent application of a yardstick. But the fact that the yardstick could not be applied did not lead to the conclusion that the distance between the earth and the sun was incapable of being measured. It just happened to be a fact that the yardstick was most easily applied when the interested observers could all be present at one time and when the measuring rod and what was to be measured could be conveniently placed side by side. This has meant that our typical mental picture of the application of a yardstick is the type of occasion on which it is most easily and most frequently used. If we have in mind that in our use of physical standards we have experience of unusual occasions when they are in principle applicable though very difficult to apply in practice, we may be more hesitant in affirming that there is no relevant moral standard in situations where its application is extremely difficult to make. Whether there is or is not a standard does not depend upon the simplicity of its application.

I said earlier that we might be mistaken not only in our basic thinking about the nature and operation of physical standards but also in the analogical language which we customarily use in thinking and speaking about them. These commonplace analogies are by no means wholly misleading but they can often mislead us if we are not fully aware that we are using them and that they are always less than perfect. I have, for example, spoken of the 'physical expressions' of the physical standard. We ought to look more carefully at this phrase. In a case of physical expression there is some physical thing which is expressed. We may, for instance, observe the gum which has been expressed or extruded through the bark of a gum-tree. Both the gum and the bark are physical materials but the gum is more plastic than the bark. Under natural pressure it is pressed through the bark and hardens when exposed to the air. The final shape of each piece of gum is determined by the natural conditions concerning the tree, the bark and the gum itself. In speaking of the expression of the gum, we may have primarily in mind the fact that it is being expressed or the physical form assumed by the gum when its expression is completed. We reach a rather different use of the word when an interior decorator is pressing some kind of plastic material out of a tube in order to fill cracks in a wall. The shape assumed by the material is determined by the shape of the orifice through which it is pressed but, in this case, the expression is the outcome of an act of will. Both the material and the tube remain physical things and the pressure is applied by the use of physical fingers, but the whole operation was designed by someone to fulfil a foreseen emergency. If we think in physical terms about expressions of the physical standards, whether we are thinking of the event or the act or the outcome, it is plain that we are running into verbal difficulties. The main problem is that a physical standard in itself is not a physical thing. Not being a physical thing, its expression cannot be fully understood in terms of a word which primarily refers to some alteration in the form of a physical thing under pressure of exceptional circumstances. In using the word, we are liable to think of the physical standard in a quasi-physical way. We tend to think of it as a physically formless thing or as a thing which has a variable physical form capable of being transformed into an infinite variety of physical expressions. We may be somewhat less misled if we draw our analogies from deliberate acts of physical expression. Here the outcome is not natural or accidental but consciously adapted to the purpose which is to be fulfilled. I have an uneasy feeling that we are using a very hazardous analogy when, in thinking of the relation between a physical standard in itself and what we call its physical expressions, we assume without hesitation that it is genuinely like an act or fact of physical expression. We may be even more mistaken when we think in this way of the relation of the moral standard to its manifold expressions. We may find ourselves gravely tempted to ask the wrong kind of questions and to expect the wrong kind

3-2

of answers. Whether we are trying to understand the expressions of physical or of other kinds of standards, we face the basic problem of appreciating how a standard can be at once distinct from and yet within its expressions; at once other than its expressions and yet in some way contained within them. It is at least clear that the mysterious status of standards, even of the simpler physical standards, cannot be adequately understood in terms of physical analogies. We shall always fail to comprehend their nature and operation if we insist on thinking of them as the ghosts of material things.

Very similar points arise if we examine the common practice of referring to the application of a standard to a particular case. This is an obscure operation which is not really very aptly described as an application. In order to see that this is so, we must recall the original sites in which the word is used and then consider its utility when used in reference to the relation between standards and the cases to which they apply. The verb 'to apply' might be called one of the pliable verbs. 'Imply', 'comply' and 'reply' are members of the same group. They all basically refer to the fact that certain physical materials are pliable. Each of them may be folded in some way, as a cloth may be folded and placed in a drawer. What has been implied can be unfolded. A material which is not rigid may be made to conform with or comply with irregular surfaces. The application of materials of this kind may be taken to mean either the process of applying or the outcome of the process. In thinking of application as an activity rather than as a state, I believe we tend to think more easily of acts of application done by people than of applications which are simply due to natural causes. With a little thought and imagination, we can conceive cases of natural application, as, for example, the way in which a tidal river as a result of an abnormally high tide may apply a thin coat of mud to areas on the banks which are not usually covered with the tidal water. We experience much less difficulty in thinking of instances where the act of application is done by a person. We can easily imagine the application of a patch to an old garment or the application of a bandage to a limb. In these cases the material is shaped or moulded to suit the circumstances. The applicant shows his art and skill in his act of applying the pliant material to the situation in which it is to be applied. It is not surprising that this easily observable and imaginable act of physical application has been taken as a source of analogies designed to describe the relation of a physical standard to a particular case. Like all analogies, it has its stronger and weaker points. It does appear reasonably apt when we envisage the application of, for instance, a yardstick to a length of material. We see two physical things which are placed together and one is taken to be the standard of measurement. It suggests a physical standard which is not attached to what is measured but conveniently capable of being placed in temporary contact with what is being measured. It suggests a standard which is independent of the circumstances to which it is relevant. All seems well. But, if even a physical standard in itself is not identical with either the process of application or its result, we are misrepresenting it if we identify it with either of these. A physical standard is not a physical thing. Even so, the analogy does suggest something of the way in which a standard stands apart from that for which it is a standard. It does not entirely fail to signify the curious distance between a standard and its application. Some indication of the independence of a standard is given in the analogy of application. But the analogy fails at the point where the absolute independence of a standard is affirmed if 'absolute' is understood in the sense of being unrelated to any circumstances whatever. The notion of the standard then becomes so diaphanous that it ceases to be distinguishable from nothing at all. A standard for nothing is not a standard. This suggests that being a standard involves being a standard for something which is the case. No standard is absolute in the sense of applying to no circumstances whatever. It is as useless as the gift of a theatre ticket which applies to no particular seat. This line of thought leads us towards the view that even a physical standard is not fully understood as applying *to* certain situations because in a sense the character of the situation affects its appropriate application. We may even speak of application which the circumstances require or demand. In any case, our study of the application of physical standards is prompting the conclusions that no standard is either identical with the situation in which it is applied or applies and that no standard is wholly without a situation in which it is relevant. The admission that our thinking even about physical standards is less than clear and distinct should make us hesitate in interpreting the moral standard in terms of the physical analogies which we employ with very moderate success in the field of physical standards. We must somehow do justice to the independence and to the relevance of the moral standard and take care that in our use of any of the traditional vocabulary we neither dismiss it as valueless nor accept it as perfect.

We have been confining our attention, perhaps unduly, to the operation of physical standards as exemplified in the metal bar at Winchester which represents the Royal Standard Yard. This had the convenience of providing a localised occasion by reference to which we could check the adequacy of the vocabulary which we were using. It provided what I believe engineers call a test-bed for the testing of a series of comparable mechanical devices. But we must not forget the great variety of other physical standards. These deserve a prolonged study in which the peculiarities of each type of physical standard could be examined, but I will simply indicate a few obvious instances. There are, for example, many standards for the quality and purity of physical materials. These are often used in regard to the quality and purity of physical materials which are manufactured, such as chemical substances that are produced in commercial quantities. As it is virtually impossible to manufacture these at a standard of absolute purity, it is customary to accept a standard of chemical purity which allows a tolerated degree of impurity. Whether a sample is up to the agreed standard is measured not by visual inspection but by some established and agreed method of chemical analysis. The standard is not represented by a standard sample which is placed alongside the material to be tested. It is expressed in a percentage and whether the sample under test exceeds this is to be ascertained by the use of an agreed procedure. It is plain that what is here called the standard of chemical purity is a complex matter including the decision to establish a standard, the decision to express it in a mathematical form, and the decision that the percentage of impurities shall be ascertained by an agreed process. There is another group of physical standards which also concern manufactured products but refer more particularly to the things which are manufactured out of the basic materials after these have been accepted as of sufficiently good quality. There are now innumerable official and unofficial standards for the safety and efficiency of all kinds of mechanical things, such as oil-heaters. These are often expressed in terms of some kind of standard unit of measurement. As we become more accustomed to this enormous increase in the use of physical standards and to the practice of physical standardisation, I believe that our conscious and unconscious understanding of the nature and operation of what we call moral standards will be affected. We may become disposed to doubt the authenticity of any type of standard which does not reproduce the admirable and convenient qualities of a physical standard.

The purpose of this lecture has been to prepare our minds for a later study of the autonomy of the moral standard. I believe that this is an essential preliminary stage in the advance towards a defence of christian theological ethics. It is essential because the notion of an autonomous moral standard combined with a belief in the autonomy of the moral agent is a central feature of the kind of secular humanism which I take to be the most serious challenge to a theological interpretation of the moral standard. If the moral standard is wholly autonomous, the major christian doctrines are bound to appear irrelevant and even open to moral objections. The precise articulation and discussion of the basic issues demand great delicacy in the use of words, particularly of the dominant words traditionally employed in the discussion. I shall examine the word 'autonomy' later, but today I have been studying the word 'standard' as it is used in the phrase 'physical standard'. I hope I have been able to show some of the ways in which we may easily misunderstand the nature and operation of these standards which we call physical. I have said that we may make the error of identifying a physical standard with its expressions or applications. In doing so, we are very liable to ignore the mystery of what is being expressed and applied. The central enigma is the nature of a standard which is in some sense other than all its expressions and applications but devoid of meaning when taken in total isolation from them. The very notion of a standard involves its relevance to situations with which it is not identical. I suggested also that we were prone to misunderstand the arbitrariness of physical standards. They were, at least in their expression and application, not arbitrary in the sense of being whimsical or capricious. Each careful expression and application was appropriate to the occasion. I made the further suggestion that the mysterious relation between a standard in itself and the forms and situations in which it was embodied was not open to any simple and direct description. Some kind of analogical description was unavoidable. The analogies of expression and application had proved their utility in surviving long usage but, like all analogies, they were by no means perfect. They could mislead us as well as assist us. The fact that we were very liable to misunderstand even physical standards was discouraging to us in our efforts to reach a true understanding of the nature of the moral standard. We were failing to understand physical standards and in danger of using our misunderstandings as the means for understanding the operation of the moral standard. We might find ourselves using bad specimens of the wrong tools.

I would have liked to pass at once to an examination of the autonomy of ethics, with special reference to the autonomy of the moral standard, but I think that a study of personal standards may teach us further lessons about the way in which the word 'standard' works before we begin to inquire in what sense a moral standard may be said to be autonomous. In philosophical theology it is a mistake to try to run before we can walk but I will try to remember that there is a difference between walking and marking time.

LECTURE 3

PERSONAL STANDARDS

It is more appropriate to think of the moral standard in terms drawn from our experience of standards in personal life.

The expression and application of the personal standards of conduct required in specified situations.

The expression of professional standards. The ways in which these are applied by professionals and the ways in which they apply to persons who are being professional.

Personal standards as the standards of being a person. The relationship of a person to the standards of his being remains mysterious. He is not identical with their expression or their application but in some way he is most himself in their true expression and true application.

PERSONAL STANDARDS

The main theme of this course of lectures is the conflict or tension between christian theological ethics and the ethics of secular humanism when it is taken for granted that both parties have a genuine respect for the moral standard and a high sense of moral responsibility. In my first lecture I suggested that the central issue was the autonomy of ethics. I took the belief in the autonomy of ethics to combine belief in the autonomy of the moral standard and a belief in the autonomy of the moral agent. These two convictions were usually associated in fact, if not of necessity. Selecting the autonomy of the moral standard as the immediate issue, I emphasised the need for care in our use of the major words traditionally employed in the discussion of these moral issues. There is nothing novel in this obvious observation but it may occasionally prompt us to undergo the chastening experience of genuinely losing confidence in the adequacy of the vocabulary which we are using. This is an experience which is distinct from recognising the inadequacy of the way in which others use their words. As long as we remain quietly convinced that our own use of words is adequate we remain blind to those rare moments of philosophic insight when the curtain of words loses something of its opacity and even, possibly, dematerialises. It therefore seemed useful to approach a study of the autonomy of ethics by a scrutiny of some of the ways in which we used the word 'standard'. In the last lecture I spoke of physical standards. I suggested that our interpretation of these was neither wholly mistaken nor free from all mistakes. We could easily be simply mistaken in our view of the nature and operation of each standard we called physical. It was in itself very elusive in not being identical with any of its expressions or applications. It was in a curious way at once outside and inside the forms in which it was expressed and applied. It was a plain error to identify a physical standard with the physical exemplar which was publicly acknowledged as a sufficient physical representation of the standard in a form which could conveniently be publicly applied. We could also be in error about our interpretation of the arbitrariness of physical standards. In some senses there was an arbitrary quality in the acts of establishing them, expressing them, and applying them, but this arbitrariness was by no means wholly a matter of caprice. Each decision was taken by a responsible person in the face of some kind of circumstances. To be a standard was to be a standard in and for certain circumstances. The notion of an absolute standard which was absolute in the sense of being totally unrelated to any environment in which it was relevant was meaningless. A standard which was completely arbitrary in the sense of standing absolutely alone was not a standard at all. It was not at all surprising that the curious relation of physical standards to their surroundings was not one which could be taken to be a relationship of physical things and therefore not one which could be adequately expressed in physical analogies. It was a relationship which in fact could not be interpreted perfectly by any analogy but it was obviously greatly misinterpreted in any thoughtless use of analogies taken from pressing one material through another or from fastening a piece of pliable material to another piece of material. These explanatory models were not wholly useless but they could easily confuse our thinking about what physical standards were and how they operated. It followed that if we were frequently misunderstanding the standards which we called physical, we were very liable to make mistakes later if we tried to understand moral standards in physical terms. There was a constant risk that we should assume that a moral standard ought to operate in the manner which we take or mistake to be characteristic of the simpler case of a physical standard. I suspect that at the moment we understand so little of either that it is something of an historical accident that we take one to be plainer than the other and therefore a suitable storehouse of explanatory analogies.

I now pass to a study of the use of the word 'standard' in the phrase 'personal standard'.

The distinction between physical and personal standards is not clear and distinct. Many cases arise where the standards may appear to be both physical and personal. In this type of case, there is a personal activity but it is of such a nature that it may be measured by some type of unit of measurement which is appropriate to physical objects and events. It is a commonplace, for example, that in the field of athletics the standards of achievement have been rising in recent years. It is worth noticing both the type of measurement which is being used and the manner in which the standard became established. We can learn from such cases useful lessons about the way in which we establish and use these standards of physical achievement. The instance of athletic standards is a fairly plain case. We all know, for example, that no man ran a mile in four minutes until a few years ago. The four-minute mile is now a recognised standard of human achievement. Unlike the standard yard, it is not a standard of convenience. It was not a triumph of human enterprise to make a decision that a yard should consist of thirty-six and not thirty-nine inches. The standard of four minutes running time for one mile was for a considerable time an unachieved target which was just beyond the limits of actual performance. When it had once been achieved, it was plain that it was a practicable, though still a most exceptional, standard. As the achievement was repeated it became the standard which the most eminent runners were expected to attain. It was in attaining the newly established standard that they themselves established their own reputations as eminent runners. There may be other cases in which other standards of athletic achievement have fallen in recent years but, in either case, the setting of the physical standard of achievement was closely related to what had actually been achieved or to what seemed to be on the point of achievement. Its final recognition by public opinion or by some athletic organisation was a conscious decision but it was not just like the decision that a yard should be of thirty-six inches. Even so, without some kind of unorganised or organised decision, there would have been no standard. The simple fact that a mile is run in four minutes and that this is known to have been done does not constitute or establish a standard. The achievement of a four-minute mile is not a standard when considered in itself. As what might be called a mere fact, it is no more a standard than the time it would take for each one of us to run a mile. (Unless in this estimate I unwittingly do any of you an injustice.) We may also note the way in which this standard of achievement happens to be expressible in terms of public units of measurement and that these units happen to be English. And we may recall that the standard is assumed to be applied in normal conditions. It is quite unnecessary to mention that the race-tracks are taken to be level and not six inches deep in soft mud. The main point is that we should recognise a class of standards of physical achievement where physical standards and personal standards are intimately combined.

We approach more closely to the complex working of personal standards if we now advance to an investigation of standards of personal behaviour. I do not have in mind at this point the great moral problems of human conduct. I want to examine in the first instance the very much simpler issues where we are all virtually agreed about the action which should be taken. In these far less disputable cases, we may see more plainly the operation of standards of personal conduct. For example, though we may differ violently about pacifism and euthanasia, I think that if smoke now began to rise from between the floor boards most of us would feel that we ought to evacuate the room in an orderly fashion and call the fire brigade. There might of course, be some proud martyr to philosophical truth who would remain quite motionless on the ground that any activity on his part would reveal an effective belief in some kind of knowable standard distinguishing between what ought and what ought not to be done. But, whatever you would propose to do or not to do, it is worth looking a little more closely at the establishment, expression and application of some standard procedure which is to be taken in case of fire. We may remind ourselves of the plain but important fact that this standard for the proper procedure is not identical with the actual procedure which is recommended or followed. The standard is other than what takes place, while being relevant to what happens. It is not identical with any of its expressions or applications. These both take the form which is appropriate in the circumstances. You will have observed that the notices in this building about the action to be taken by anyone discovering a fire are understandably brief. They have a brevity which suits the occasion. They include no dissertation upon the nature of fire which would delight the heart of a natural scientist. You are not told how to recognise a fire when you see one. The actions proposed are plainly related to the time at your disposal and to the circumstances of the emergency. It is rightly assumed that you would supplement the brief expressions of the standard procedure by the exercise of your common sense. The advice to telephone the fire station implies that you should use the nearest available telephone and no saving clause is added that if the nearest telephone is already known by you to be out of action, you are to assume that the verb 'telephone' means that you should use the telephone which is at once nearest and also in working order. At point after point you are expected to display sound judgement in the application of the standard which has been briefly and compactly communicated to you through its expression in the official notice. I hope that this example will serve to show us the confusions which will arise if, in thinking of any standard of personal behaviour, we fail to draw any distinction between the standard in itself and its changing expression and application in changing situations.

There is a further obvious but most important point that the activity of the agent is always related to what is the case at the time that he acts. What is the case includes a vast variety of facts of many different types. I cannot at this point enter into an extended examination of this phrase but I will indicate something of the variety of so-called facts which constitute a case. If a case is taken to be a case of what might have been otherwise, the total facts of the case must include the conditions and context within which alternative cases were possible. The case in itself is an abstraction. The limits of each actual case which has befallen are a matter of decision and not of observation. One of the facts of the case is that the agent in his conscious action is always bound to act on what he takes to be the facts of the case. He acts on the basis of the case as known to him at the time of action. He cannot consciously act in the light of what he does not know. His action is affected by what he happens to know of the appropriate standard and by what he knows of the situation in which it is to be observed. The standard is known to him by means of the expression which he has in mind and his application of the standard is affected by what he honestly believes to be the facts of the case. The perennial difficulty is that he may be honestly mistaken about the facts. He may be acting under an innocent misapprehension. Let me take a simple illustration. An historian, having taken every reasonable precaution, relies upon the evidence of a letter which is later shown to be a forgery. When he relied upon the letter, he had no reasonable ground for doubting its authenticity. He was in a state of what is somewhat unhappily called invincible ignorance. His professional integrity therefore remains untarnished. These obvious points should be in our minds when we are thinking of what we call the application of any standard of personal behaviour to any actual cases of personal activity. If we are not to misunderstand what is the case when a personal standard is being applied we must not forget that a supremely important fact in the case is what the agent assumes to be the case. His eventual activity is affected by the conditions of all his activity and by the factual accuracy of what he takes to be these conditions. It requires more than confidence to walk successfully on very thin ice.

I think we may deepen our insight into the nature and operation of personal standards if we give some consideration to those standards which are acknowledged and observed by people who are recognised as professionals. They have their personal professional standards. We speak, for example, without hesitation of professional historians or professional scientists. We are confident that they recognise and obey the appropriate standards in their professional activities. They are known as good historians or good scientists. Their work is governed by professional standards. Now, it is far easier to say that these professionals have their professional standards than to understand the nature and operation of these standards and the manner in which they may be expressed and applied. There is the constant danger of interpreting them in terms of physical standards and of thinking that we have understood them when we say that they differ from the standards which are physical. We have not understood how an electric current flows through a wire if we know that it does not do so exactly as a fluid might flow through a tube. Recognition of ignorance may be a useful preparation for knowledge but it is not a substitute. We must also notice at once that these professional standards of the historian and the scientist are not identical with the attitudes and activities to which they are relevant. The standards always stand in some sense apart from what is done without ceasing to be precisely relevant to what is done. But we cannot assume without more ado that a professional standard must stand apart from that to which it refers in exactly the same manner in which physical standards of measurement and achievement stand to whatever is subject to them. We must always be ready to interpret the nature and operation of new types of standards in explanatory terms and forms other than those which we have previously found useful in what we have taken to be comparable circumstances. And we must also notice that though in some senses these professional standards are arbitrarily determined, they are not arbitrary in the sense of being no more than matters of whim and fancy. They embody the lessons of experience. They have been discovered in the actual business of writing good history and of doing good science. They are related to the capacities of the human mind as engaged in historical and scientific research and they are closely related to the character of the actual world in which historical and scientific inquiry are both practicable and practised. But we must not proceed to suppose that the responsible arbitrariness of professional standards is always exactly like the deliberate arbitrariness of the physical standards of measurement and achievement.

We observed that the expression of the standard procedure to be followed in case of fire was rightly brief and practical. In the expression of professional standards there is no similar need for brevity and immediate practicality. In the recurrent situations which face a professional historian or scientist, there are many opportunities for fuller and more precisely formulated expressions of what is called the professional standard. This phrase covers many very diverse expressions of the standards which a professional must accept and practise. We naturally find ourselves speaking of the standards rather than of a single standard. The use of the plural comes naturally to our minds. No single expression is sufficient and there is no need to compress the whole standard into a single expression. A plurality of expressions is a characteristic of the personal standards which are professional. Each mode of expression is intimately related to one of the manifold types of situation which meet a professional in the course of his work. Each expression is related to the circumstances of its use. The vast variety of ways in which professional standards are expressed is bound to give an impression of untidiness. They form no system, except in a very loose sense. I will simply mention a variety of forms in which the professional may express his standards. He may formulate a series of general principles which cover many cases. These principles of action give most practical guidance when they cover a limited number of cases and provide almost no guidance when they are so generalised as to cover a vast range of cases. A professional historian who is in doubt about some matter of professional conduct is not helped by being advised to act like an historian. This advice is at once impeccable and almost useless. He may also be guided by a careful attention to the precedents established in earlier comparable cases. He may learn a deeper understanding of his professional standards both from commonplace cases and from those rare but significant cases which illustrate some disputed point. At other times, his standard may present itself to him as recollections of the advice and directions which he received when he was undergoing his professional training. There may be a set of rules which he remembers or a variety of techniques and attitudes which he learnt from working alongside those who were more expert than himself. He may be both consciously and unconsciously influenced by the tradition of the historical community to which he belongs. He may be a recognisable representative of a particular school of historical writing or show the typical characteristics of the pupils of some famous training establishment. His standard may be more properly described as an attitude or a policy rather than as a systematic body of rules and regulations. At present I myself see no good reason for claiming that a professional standard is most truly expressed in any single form of expression. As a personal standard it has a quality of infinity which is never wholly contained in any of the types and instances of expression which have been devised to meet an endless variety of comparable but never completely similar situations.

In our own age there is an increasing realisation of the need to express professional personal standards in forms which lie between particular precepts for particular cases and general rules which are so general as to yield little or no particular guidance. The awareness of this need is shown in the astonishing growth of professional codes of conduct. These are no longer limited to a few famous codes for the traditional professions. They now extend to a very large number of human occupations which are progressing towards professional status. Hardly a week goes by without some reference in the press to some kind of code of conduct for a body of men engaged in the same trade or occupation. Like the Highway Code these expressions of a professional standard include both wide generalisations and more particular guidance on what the members of the profession know to be awkward issues. They seldom offer a whole system of professional ethics but they express a more practical and pragmatic approach to the whole question of the growth and establishment of the standards which should characterise members of a profession.

The fact that professional standards may be expressed in such a diversity of ways should not lead us to conclude that every professional act is done with conscious reference to some explicit formulation of the standard. A great deal of the best professional work is done by those to whom the observance of high professional standards has become second nature. They maintain a high standard of professional work without any conscious concern about the standard which they are upholding. It is observed but not by a series of acts of conscious observation. There is no anxious search for an adequate expression of the standard which may then be laboriously applied. Awareness of the standard which has been observed may come in a fleeting moment of satisfaction when a piece of work is completed or when an expert spectator utters a word of professional admiration. The labour of finding suitable expressions of the standard and of deliberately devising appropriate applications is more likely to be a conscious burden in moments of doubt and hesitation. A good historian and a good scientist are able, if challenged, to express and discuss the standards which they accept and employ, but they may be quite unconscious of these while they actually engage in historical or scientific work. They are like accomplished pianists the perfection of whose playing no longer betrays the practice which made the playing perfect.

Problems about the working of personal standards are by no means limited to questions about the forms in which they may appropriately be expressed. Equally great, if not greater, problems arise concerning their application. The act, for instance, of applying a professional standard may be easily misunderstood. We may speak of applying some expression of the professional standard as though our action was just like the application of a yardstick to a piece of cloth. This is a mistake. Let us take the example of applying a professional principle. There could be a conscientious historian who on principle refused to accept any evidence from a certain private diary except when it could be corroborated from a more trustworthy source. If we look more carefully at the use made of this principle we shall see that it is incorrect to say that it is applied by the historian. He does whatever he does. He does not do the principle. He cannot do a principle because all action is particular. What he does is in accord with his principle of action. The principle is only applied in the sense that it is allowed to govern his actions. No principle is ever applied as the physical expression of what we call a physical standard is applied to a physical situation for which it is a standard. I believe that we should find the same to be true of every conceivable expression of a professional standard. Each is used as some kind of guide to what is done. The expression is not itself applied. Professional attitudes are no more applied than professional principles, if we interpret the act of application as being just like, or even very like, the act of applying the replica of a physical standard. It is quite essential that in any study of the expression and application of a professional standard we should try to look through the traditional terminology towards what we can discern of what is actually taking place.

In my study of various ways in which personal standards may be said to be expressed or applied, there has been one serious omission. Up to this point, our study of personal standards has been primarily concerned with professional standards and much of our attention has been given to the act of applying a professional standard to a situation. We have been specially interested in the expression of a standard and its application by a professional in any particular situation. We have often been concerned to notice the way in which the notion of a standard apart from any situation for which it is a proper standard quickly loses all meaning. We have been observing the intricate ways in which a standard is related to its expressions and applications but we have not given our central attention to the applicant himself in the act of expressing and applying his professional standards. This omission may have been partly accidental. When we envisage a situation requiring professional activity, we may place ourselves at the standpoint of the agent who acts, or of the patient who is affected by the act, or of a spectator who is not directly involved in the case as agent or patient. What we see of what we take to be the case is deeply affected by our standpoint and our interest in the case. If we identify ourselves with the agent we fail to see him, as, for example, a photographer, in the absence of special devices, fails to appear in the group of people whom he photographs. And, if we identify ourselves with the patient or the spectator, we may still be primarily interested in the way the standard is handled and applied than in its relation to the applicant. To this matter we must now turn. But in examining more carefully the way in which a professional standard applies to a professional we must try not to forget what we have noticed about the application of a professional standard to a situation. We realise, for instance, that professional standards are not only applied by an historian; they apply to him. In saying that professional standards apply to a professional man, we mean more than that they happen to apply to him. We do not mean that they apply as someone might apply a yardstick to a length of cloth or to a table top. In these cases, the physical replica of the physical standard has no essential association with what is measured. The two physical things may be put together or taken apart as the circumstances demand. The relation of a professional standard to a professional man is something very different. We misunderstand both him and his standard if we take each as fully existing in isolation from the other. His relationship to his proper professional standards is not a matter of accident or whim. A person is not a professional before he decides to accept the established professional standards. It is in his acceptance and practice of them that he becomes a professional. A person is not a professional scientist before he recognises the professional standards of his profession. An historian is not a professional historian prior to his acknowledgement of the standards which are essential in an historian. Moreover, a person does not become a genuine professional when he accepts the standards for some reason other than his own belief in their excellence as professional standards. A person cannot be made a true historian or scientist by force or bribery. His conversion to an acceptance of the right standards cannot be under duress or for the sake of material reward. He must freely identify himself with the kind of person who admits and employs the proper standards of his profession. He is not a professional apart from the professional standards which he holds. He is constituted an historian or a scientist in the act of accepting them. It is even somewhat misleading to speak of the act of accepting them. This is not like the act of accepting a medal. It is rather the passive act of accepting the fact that to be a professional historian or a professional scientist involves accepting the proper standards. It is an act of discovering what it means to be a member of these professions. It is an act of professional self-awareness. What we mistakenly call an act is essentially mysterious because it appears that a person is unable to appreciate what it means to be a professional before he has become one. There is no simple continuity between the state of being an unprofessional person and becoming a professional person. The transition has something of the character of a conversion or a new creation. The new professional insights and loyalties are neither wholly new nor are they simply a deepening of insights already possessed. There is some kind of discontinuity between the old and the new. Each flash of insight into the real meaning of being a professional is a moment of fascinating growth. Professional being is coming into being; the creation of a professional is taking place.

I chose to illustrate some of the features of personal standards from the examples of the professional historians and scientists because it may reasonably be claimed that they both employ methods and standards which have received a considerable degree of definition and refinement. There are many other personal standards which are less clearly articulated. They have not received that degree of clarity in expression and conventionality in application which makes it possible for them to be compactly described and communicated. It is obviously much more difficult to formulate the professional standards of a good surgeon or a good novelist. Those who believe that there is a genuine distinction between good and bad novelists are bound to believe that some kind of standard is being or not being acknowledged and practised. This recognition does not imply, however, that any adequate expression of this standard is available or that its precise method of application is fully known. The manifest difficulties in expressing and applying many types of professional standards should not be taken as immediate proof that there are no standards to be expressed or applied. The fact that personal standards cannot be as conveniently operated as the physical standards which can be represented in some physical replica does not show that belief in personal standards must be an illusion.

If it be true that a person becomes a professional in accepting and using the standards which are proper to his profession, we may be prompted to ask whether being a person involves the acceptance and use of personal standards. I think this may well be so. I cannot think that a person is a person prior to acknowledging and applying the standards of life and thought which are characteristic of being a person. If, for example, thinking is a characteristic of a personal being, in what sense is anyone a person who refuses to accept the principle of contradiction? The necessary result of rejecting this principle is that logical thinking becomes an impossibility. The penalty of refusing the principle is that no logical thought can take place. This suggests that a person does not adopt a standard of consistent thought as he might adopt one of the standard methods of cleaning silver. He displays and finds his being as a person in living in harmony with the standards of personal being. A person is a being with personal standards; apart from these standards he is not a person. He may be said to apply them but the deeper matter is that they apply to him. He may choose not to apply them but he cannot by an act of his own will dissociate himself from their application to him. It is in recognising and practising them that he is discovering his own true being. In so far as he fails to recognise them and is careless in applying them, he is losing touch with what he truly is.

In the present lecture I have touched on so many points about the nature and operation of personal standards that we are in danger of losing sight of the general course which we have been following. The purpose of this lecture was to continue our study of the ways in which the word 'standard' is used. It was part of our preparation for a study of the autonomy of ethics. In the last lecture I sought to show some of the typical characteristics of physical standards and today I have invited you to consider some of the curious features of the standards which we call personal. I suggested or implied at a number of points that we were both helped and hindered by our natural inclination to interpret the logical behaviour of the vocabulary of personal standards in terms of our experience of the standards which we called physical. As in the case of physical standards, we faced the perennial mystery of the way in which a standard is at once other than and relevant to whatever is subject to the standard. This mysterious relationship might be clarified a little if we realised that, in speaking of a standard, the speaker might have in mind the standard in itself or the standard in its expressions or applications. I have tried to show that we fail to observe the truth of the matter if we seek to think of the standard in itself, in the sense of being out of all relation to any circumstances whatever, or if we seek to identify the standard with its expressions and applications. These were always less than the standard itself but they were not wholly arbitrary or haphazard. Each expression presented the standard in a form which could be conveniently used by morally responsible people in the business of making personal decisions about what should be done. I did not attempt to give any kind of exhaustive list of possible types of expressions of our personal standards but I did want to emphasise the danger of identifying our standards with any of its expressions. I said rather more about the application of personal standards because this operation is far from clear. It is certainly not just like applying the physical replica of a physical standard to a piece of physical material. Amongst the many points about the application of personal standards which might have been emphasised, I selected three for more detailed investigation. In the first place, it is strictly misleading to say that we apply the expressions of our personal standards. When we act with some measure of deliberation, we may envisage what we propose to do or we may accept some principle of action but what we actually do is a particular act in time and space. We do not do our mental picture of what might be done; we do not do any principle which we may have adopted. In the second place, each application of a personal standard is to the facts of the case in so far as these are known at the time of acting. It is a most significant fact in each case that the agent acts on what he takes to be the facts of the case and on many occasions he may be simply mistaken about the facts. One of the facts of any case of personal conduct is that the agent is always acting in some measure of ignorance. In the third place, I reminded you that we failed to see the whole operation of application if we looked only at the way in which people applied their standards to the situations in which they found themselves. There was also the curious way in which personal standards, as for instance in the form of professional standards, applied to those who applied them. A professional was not a professional when not accepting and practising the standards which are proper to his profession. It looked as though a person could not be a person quite apart from the personal standards which properly apply to a person. These standards are not simply held by a person but they hold of any being which we are willing to call personal.

I hope that some of these points may assist us later in our major task of interpreting christian theological ethics in a manner which does justice to what is true in the ethics of secular humanism and offers some answers to various problems which the secularist may often overlook. At least, I may have made you thoroughly tired of the word 'standard'. This would be progress, because I believe that one of the most effective factors in the progress of philosophical theology is the promotion of sheer boredom with any traditional or contemporary jargon. Even so, some of you may legitimately think that the type of boredom which I induce is not the specifically creative boredom which is so greatly to be desired.

LECTURE 4

THE AUTONOMY OF ETHICS

This phrase is taken to include both the autonomy of the moral standard and the autonomy of the moral agent.

To be autonomous originally means the ability and freedom to make and to obey one's own laws.

The rather curious analogical use of this adjective in describing (i) the moral standard as 'autonomous', (ii) the moral agent as 'autonomous'.

Though these analogical uses of the term may be useful, they can be misleading. Their use must be controlled by our experience of living under the moral standard, including our experience of moral failure and moral progress.

THE AUTONOMY OF ETHICS

'The Autonomy of Ethics' is an almost unintelligible phrase but we cannot avoid the labour of trying to understand it by the simple expedient of ceasing to use it. It is too well established to be ignored and in its own obscure way it does refer to a central issue in the debate between secular and christian moralists when both are accepting the autonomy of the moral standard and the autonomy of the moral agent.[1] It is the acceptance of these autonomies which causes the main moral problems and misgivings about the legitimacy of christian theological ethics. It does so easily appear that a genuinely autonomous moral standard not only requires no theological support but is degraded in accepting any such assistance. And a genuine autonomy of the moral agent raises real moral problems about the possibility and propriety of accepting the help of divine grace. No defence of theological ethics against the moral criticisms which are made by this group of conscientious secular moralists can leave unexamined what may be meant when ethics are said to be autonomous.

The two previous lectures on physical and personal standards have been an attempt to prepare our minds for this investigation of autonomy as ascribed to the moral standard and the moral agent. I thought it was sounder to begin by considering what might possess some kind of autonomy than to consider autonomy as such and then search for whatever might possess it. Even the tailor of

[1] Cf. *Prospect for Metaphysics*, ed. I. T. Ramsey (1961), essay 2.

ready-made suits would admit that despite the usefulness of his profession the most fitting result is reached when the shape of the individual customer is allowed to determine the shape of the suit. Suits which were simply designed as such would be both an exacting enterprise in the art of suit-designing and, in any case, unlikely to find a wholly satisfied wearer. If we are to profit by our earlier studies of the nature and operation of physical and personal standards, I think we must spend a little time recording some of the points which I hope have become clear. What are the results of our inquiry so far? I will try to enumerate as plainly and simply as I can some of the conclusions which I have reached, though whether you accept them is, of course, quite another matter. I do not believe that any standard is identical with its form of expression. Physical standards are frequently represented in some form of physical exemplar but the exemplar is not the standard in itself. The yard as an official unit of length is not the same as the yardstick. Our personal standards are also not identical with their expressions. The brief instructions about what is to be done in case of fire are only a partial expression of what is required and even where the standard is expressed it is not identical with the physical print on the notices. There are greater opportunities of expressing in fuller and more precise forms those personal standards which are the standards of professionals but the standard itself is never exhaustively expressed in any of them. And I do not believe that any standard is identical with its application, whether this is understood as the act of applying or the state of having been applied. There is a certain irreducible distance between a standard and its application.

But this curious distance must not be exaggerated. Though standards are not identical with their expressions or their applications, they are not at such a distance from them as to be wholly irrelevant. It is not possible to have a standard which stands as a standard for no circumstances whatever. The difficulty is to conceive of standards which are at once above and within their expressions and applications. It is quite understandable that their detachment from these is often interpreted as a capacity for making arbitrary decisions about the modes of expression and application but this is very different from any irresponsible caprice. Each expression, including, of course, the more traditional forms, is formulated for use in particular circumstances. The same standard may be expressed in a particular precept or in a more general principle. That is, the freedom of expression is exercised in actual situations in an actual world which permits the expression of different types of standards in different ways. Somewhat similarly the arbitrariness in the application of standards is not unlimited but related to the kinds of application which the actual world allows. There are no impossible actual applications of a standard. When a standard is being expressed or applied there is the further important point that these acts are performed by agents who at the time of action necessarily act upon what they believe to be the case about the world in which they act. There may be a serious discrepancy between what is actually so and what they take to be so. Many famous last words have proved to be the last because they were spoken in ignorance of what was actually the case. Our thinking and speaking about the nature and status of standards are also liable to be confused by the use of a vocabulary which was originally devised to deal with matters which were not matters of morality. The physical analogies of expression and application can be misleading. For example, in speaking of the application of a personal standard we are very likely to suppose that a personal standard is applied as one may apply a physical tape measure to some physical material which is being measured. This is a mistake. We are being led astray by the language which we are using. We fail, for example, to see the important distinction between a person applying his professional standards and the way in which his professional standards apply to him as a professional. There are two types of application here which must not be confused though they are closely related. Each is misunderstood if we describe them by a careless use of analogies drawn from physical situations. These are the kinds of considerations which we ought to have in mind when we turn to look at the strange autonomies of moral standards and moral agents.

In speaking of the moral standard and the moral agent as autonomous the general impression is given that they are in some way unrestricted or independent. A status is being ascribed to them which is free from any kind of alien or external control. Though this is the generally accepted meaning of the word, it is plain that we must examine this rather general meaning to discover whether it conceals a variety of meanings. We must notice some of the different senses in which something may be said to be autonomous. We are bound to become confused in our discussion of the autonomy of ethics if we carelessly use the same word with different meanings. We must first recall the primary site in which the word is used and proceed to study its various transferred and derivative uses. We are likely to find that some of these are somewhat strained and forced. They remind me of what happens when an ancient city church is demolished and parts of the stonework and internal furnishings are incorporated in a newly built church on a housing estate in the suburbs. In some way the features from the old church represent a continuity with the past and effectively fulfil a renewed function in the present but it usually remains evident that they were not initially designed for the new positions in which they are placed. Or, to put the point in another way, it might be said that many of our transferred words always give an impression of that pathetic homelessness which is associated with displaced persons. We may, therefore, begin by asking, what was the original site or homeland of the word 'autonomy'? Its most direct use is to describe a situation where a personal being is living under his own laws. This autonomy may be possessed by a corporate body or by an individual. When these are autonomous, they are free to live under the laws which they themselves have made. The basic autonomy is the ability and freedom to establish the laws under which they are going to live. The authority to establish their own laws includes the authority to revise and revoke them. They are autonomous in that they legislate for themselves without being subject to any control by some higher authority. To possess this kind of authority and capacity is to possess autonomy in its simplest and most direct sense.

This legislative freedom is a complex matter. It is part of the whole mystery of human freedom. Those who believe that the moral agent is in some sense free to determine his future conduct believe that one of the many ways of expressing his intentions is the use of rules or laws. These expressions of his free will in a legal form are by no means limited to acts of legislation by public bodies. The essence of any legal expression of a human will is that it refers to a number of similar cases in which a decision about human conduct is likely to be required. It does not refer to one case only. It includes or covers a number of comparable cases. If I make it a rule to start my work each day at nine o'clock, I am not simply deciding to begin at that hour on a single occasion but on all future working days. In itself a legislative decision may seem quite a simple operation but it loses this superficial simplicity when we begin to observe the vast range of conditions which make the decision possible and the great variety of subsidiary or associated decisions which are contained within the main act of decision. If we are to see something of this complexity, we are bound to analyse the situation and to treat what we have analysed in quite artificial isolation. This study of autonomous legislative power is not unlike the study of the human body. We know, for example, that it is convenient to study the digestive system apart from the circulation of the blood, but we also know that the body is a living whole which is greatly misrepresented when its various functionings are examined apart from one another. It would be ideal to think of everything at once but most of us are better at thinking of one thing at a time. I think we are more likely to advance towards a fuller understanding of our legislative autonomy if we adopt the distinctions which I drew when in the earlier lectures

I was considering the nature and operation of physical and personal standards. I shall, therefore, consider the exercise of legislative autonomy in three phases, first the establishment of laws, second, the expression of laws, and third, the application of laws. Various types of autonomy may be exercised in each of these distinguishable but not separable enterprises. I hope that in this way we may find ourselves in a better position to realise what we mean when we say that the moral standard or the moral agent is autonomous.

To say that someone is autonomous in the sense of being free and able to establish his own laws suggests that he is free to establish whatever laws he may choose. It sounds as though his autonomy is absolute. This is a mistake. There is no absolute legislative autonomy in the sense of freedom to legislate without any regard to any circumstances whatever. A strictly absolute autonomy would be quite unrelated to what was the case about both the legislator and his world. Legislative autonomy is not a meaningless omnipotence. All actual autonomy is exercised within the conditions which make its exercise possible. If we are to make progress in understanding the conditional character of actual autonomy, we must look more closely at the types of conditions which affect its exercise. We may learn something from our experience of the way in which rules are established for various kinds of outdoor games. We know, for instance, that the rules of hockey and the rules of association football differ considerably though both games involve the use of a ball and goals. Each of these games has a governing body which is autonomous in the sense of being free and able to promulgate official rules for the game and to revise these from time to time. It might seem that this legislative autonomy was absolute but it is evident that the character of the rules is related to the conditions in which the game is possible. The size of the pitch is determined by the physical capacities of the players and by the permitted means of moving the ball from place to place. The rules are closely related to the circumstances in which it is possible to play the game. They remain, of course, hypothetical imperatives in the sense that there is no need to participate in the game if you do not wish to do so. At a deeper level the possibility of outdoor games is related to the facts of the natural order. If the normal laws of gravity did not apply, neither the players nor the ball would remain in the field of play. Without a stable natural order, it would not be possible to exercise autonomy in establishing the characteristic rules of any outdoor game. Although in one sense the regularities of nature are a limitation upon the autonomy of those who legislate for the games, they may also be considered as the conditions without which the legislative autonomy would be meaningless. A different type of limitation upon freedom to legislate may be the subordination of one law-making body to another. The inferior or local legislator may enjoy legislative freedom but only within a restricted area, for example, a national authority which controls the rules of a game as played within the boundaries of the nation may have no power to establish rules for other countries. I need not pursue this illustration further if I have been able to remind you that every autonomous legislator is exercising what is in some senses a conditional autonomy.

Within the limiting conditions the legislator may enjoy

considerable freedom of action but it is a mistake to think that this freedom is bound to be used in a capricious way. Arbitrary decisions need not be irresponsible. One of the most important characteristics of a responsible use of legislative autonomy is the exercise of special care in learning and accepting the conditions in which it is possible to legislate. It is a mark of irresponsibility if the legislator knowingly acts beyond his powers in the hope that his transgressions will not be noticed. And it is a mark of ignorance on the part of the legislator if he mistakes the limits within which he may properly legislate.

Very similar points might be made about the type of autonomy which a legislator may exercise in selecting the form in which his legislative will is to be expressed. Each law which he establishes is not expressed in general but in some quite particular expression. Usually, the expression is in the form of words but this is not always so. An arrow chalked on a wall is an instance of a command or invitation to follow a certain direction without these being expressed in words. We noticed earlier when examining the operation of physical and personal standards that they were at once other than their expressions while being in some way expressed in them. And we also noticed that the expressions which they assumed were conveniently adapted to the situations in which the standard was being in some sense applied. A yardstick was, for example, a very suitable instrument for measuring in yards, and personal standards were expressed in a great diversity of forms which were appropriate for use on different occasions as guides to personal conduct. The expression of a personal will in the form of a law is a good example of the selection

77

of a particular form on the ground of its utility. The legal form is useful in various ways. It is a labour-saving device in that an established rule saves the labour of treating each case as a wholly novel case. The guidance incorporated in a legal form covers or includes a group of comparable cases. The law is also a convenient vehicle for transmitting a tradition of individual or social conduct. As a command it provides direction for any series of situations which resemble one another. At a deeper level the custom of expressing a personal will in a legal form may indicate a profound desire to believe that the behaviour of an individual or a society is capable of being expressed in a manner which is ultimately rationally coherent; that what is done should be capable of being interpreted as a systematic enterprise and not simply as an assembly of unrelated decisions. It is not surprising that the legislator who rejoices in a legal expression of his will is often a stout defender of the place of reason in ethics. But it would be a mistake, in recollecting the utility of the expression of a personal will in a legal form, if we forgot that many other forms of expression are available. A recognisable personal attitude or policy may be most valuable without being expressed in any series of rules and regulations. A personal example may shine more effectively than a rule which may make no appeal to the imagination. In short, the will of the autonomous legislator may express itself not only in establishing a law but in choosing to express it in some type of legal form and in selecting the particular individual expression which he believes to be the most appropriate in each particular set of circumstances.

Great patience is needed in conducting any act of dissection and I have already, I fear, stretched both your patience and my own in making an examination of some of the ways in which the word 'autonomy' is used. But this is unfortunately not a sufficient reason for leaving the task uncompleted. We must finally look carefully at the autonomy of the agent in the sense of his freedom in applying the rule or law which has been established and expressed in some kind of legal form. We must consider how these are applied. I think that our earlier study of the application of physical and personal standards may help us to avoid a number of mistakes. Recalling that neither a physical nor a personal standard is identical with its expression or application, we can refuse the temptation to identify any personal standard with the legal form in which it happens to be expressed. And we may recall that it is not strictly true to say that any expression of a personal standard is directly applied to any particular case. The principle or law is applied only in the sense that it is used as a guide to what is done. Law is not done but kept. And we may also remember that personal standards in the form of principles or maxims were seen to apply in two senses. They may be recognised and accepted by the agent as applying to him, in the sense that he knows that he would cease to be truly himself if he disregarded them. They are applicable to him in the sense that he finds them to apply whether he desires them to do so or not. In a second sense, the legal expressions are applied by the agent to the various situations in which he has to make a decision.

If we have these points in mind, we may be disposed to consider the autonomy of the agent in the application of personal standards, when these are expressed in the form of laws, as a special case of the more general problem concerning the way a personal being may guide his conduct by reference to some expression of the elusive standard which in itself always remains in and beyond the manifold expressions it receives.

We undertook this analysis of the various ways of understanding the meaning of autonomy in order to prepare our minds for an unprejudiced study of the phrase 'the autonomy of ethics'. We were unlikely to avoid mistakes in understanding the autonomy of the moral agent and the autonomy of the moral standard if we assumed without examination that the word had the same meaning in both cases. We can now see that it is used differently in the two cases. The autonomy of the moral agent may refer to his autonomy as a legislator or to his autonomy in expressing his laws or in applying the laws which he has made or recognised as the laws of his being. I think this diversity of meaning is overlooked in the everyday references to the moral agent's autonomy. The commonplace understanding is limited to his freedom in obeying or in disobeying whatever type of legal form the standards of his personal conduct have assumed. His autonomy is usually taken to mean his moral freedom, which is the basis of his being subject to praise or blame. This is undeniably a major interpretation of the autonomy possessed by a moral agent but it is not a complete account of the diversity of autonomies which he is exercising or of the conditions within which they are exercised. The moral standard cannot be autonomous in the senses in which a moral agent may be autonomous. The reason is that a personal being may have some kind of capacity to establish, to express and to apply some kind of standard expressed in some kind of legal form, but a moral standard which in itself is devoid of any personal characteristics is incapable of establishing, or expressing, or applying itself. An impersonal standard is unable to function in any of these ways. It does not possess the various autonomies which are characteristic of an autonomous legislator.

But we must restrain the vehemence of our attack upon the literal impropriety of saying that the moral standard is autonomous. It is an undeniable fact of experience that this adjective has been used and found useful for many years. It would not have survived if it had not fulfilled some useful function. It has retained its popularity because it has been a convenient analogical description of the independence of the moral standard. In saying that it is autonomous the conviction has been expressed that this standard requires no extraneous support or approval. It does not need and, in fact, morally excludes, any divine basis or divine approbation. For example, if we witness a piece of wanton cruelty, we are all outraged. We naturally protest. We say that it is intolerable. We assert that it ought not to have been done; that it is simply not permissible for a human being to act in this way. If we speak in this way we are talking as though there were some kind of law against wanton cruelty. We are interpreting the operation of the moral standard as analogous to the operation of a human law. And we are affirming that the moral standard is autonomous, in the sense of being a law which we cannot set aside. It is as if it had the capacity and authority to make a law which we may disobey but never abrogate. It was, I believe, in this way that it became habitual to describe the moral standard as autonomous, though I myself find it a very awkward use of the word.

Now I agree that in the heat of the moment while we are witnessing an act of wanton cruelty we are very likely to condemn it without any conscious reference to the existence or will of God. The act is simply seen as something which ought not to be taking place. It can be seen to be wrong by those who no longer believe the christian faith and by christians without any conscious act of exploring the practical implications of their faith. At first glance, the moral standard which is outraged by an act of wanton cruelty does not seem to need any kind of theological support. And, on reflection, there are the moral misgivings about theological ethics which I mentioned in my opening lecture. But in the discussion of any problem in philosophical ethics there is always a risk in appealing to what are claimed to be exemplary cases. It is not a mistake to appeal to cases of moral experience, but it is misleading if we fail to examine carefully the precise significance of the case which has been selected or if we fail to observe other cases which may occur to us on further reflection. In supporting an argument by reference to cases, there is a tendency to select those which are favourable to our contention and to overlook those which are less favourable.

When we witness an act of wanton cruelty which offends against what we call the autonomy of the moral standard, we may be interpreting this autonomy in one of two ways. We may be limiting ourselves to a plain matter of reporting that we find what is being done to be inconsistent with what we believe to be the moral standard. We are doing no more than giving an account of the fact that we find this inconsistency. When we speak in this way no claim is being made that anyone else ought to feel as we feel. We are giving a report of our own attitude without suggesting or asserting that all other human beings ought to share our attitude. In the second interpretation much more is being asserted. In saying that the act is contrary to the moral standard we are affirming that all others ought to share our judgement of the case. We are doing more than informing others of what happens to be our private opinion of the case. We are contending that the moral standard has autonomy in the sense that it can be seen in the case under observation to be against a rule or law which no human will can set aside. We are acknowledging that an individual may fail to observe the standard but we are not admitting that he is autonomous in the sense that he can set the standard aside. In the first case we are saying that we find it impossible not to condemn an act of wanton cruelty; in the second case we are saying that in witnessing an act of wanton cruelty we find ourselves affirming that it offends against a moral standard which has autonomy or sovereignty over all men.

The second interpretation is conscientiously held by the kind of secular moralist who has misgivings about christian theological ethics. He believes in a moral standard which may often be expressed in the form of a law. I share his belief in a moral standard which cannot be set aside by the will of man. I begin to diverge from him when we approach the problem of understanding the status and operation of a moral standard which is admitted to be autonomous. At the moment when the wantonly cruel act was observed, there may well have been neither the time nor the inclination to reflect upon the philosophical problems involved in a just appreciation of the standing of the standard which we knew to be outraged. But problems which may be overlooked in the heat of the moment do not disappear by being disregarded. Once the judgement is made, whether implicitly or explicitly, that the moral standard possesses autonomy in the sense of being independent of any human will, we cannot avoid the questions which arise about the best way of understanding a standard which has so many curious and contrary characteristics. Let us recall some of these. We know that there are no absolute standards in the sense of being absolutely out of touch with every possible type of situation. A standard for nothing is not a standard at all. And we know that every standard is somehow other than the expressions in which it is expressed. We also know that a standard is at one and the same time other than yet exactly relevant to the situations which are subject to it. These intractable problems are not answered by any mere repetition of the affirmation that the moral standard is autonomous. The problem is to conceive of it in a way which does justice to the paradoxical characteristics which it possesses. The difficulty of this enterprise is intensified because we are always inclined to think in terms drawn from the vocabulary which we have found useful in thinking about physical and personal standards. These earlier vocabularies are still useful but they suffer from serious deficiencies when they are thoughtlessly applied to the interpretation of the status of the moral standard. It is simply misleading to think of it as just like the physical exemplar of a physical standard or as just like the private will of a good man. It is in the sheer absence of any really satisfactory explanations of the nature of the moral standard that we may feel compelled to turn in the later lectures to a fresh examination of christian theological ethics, which, without rejecting what is true in secular ethics, may offer a more profound interpretation of the autonomy of the moral standard.

I mentioned earlier that, though the autonomy of the moral agent properly means his capacity to legislate, the more general meaning of the word has been the freedom of the agent to obey or to disobey the moral law. It is this moral freedom which is analogically described as an autonomy. And it is in view of this freedom that the agent is the subject of praise or blame. He is praiseworthy when he exercises his freedom in doing what he knows to be his duty and he is blameworthy when he neglects it. His freedom is usually taken to be the basis of his responsibility. He is accountable for his actions because they are assumed to be under his control. I take this to be the general outlook of the kind of secular moralist whom I have in mind. It is this belief which is the basis of the moral misgivings which have been expressed about the propriety of divine grace whether given or received. On this view it appeared that no moral agent could be given credit for any action which was not due to his own effort and enterprise. No doubt, in cases of simple moral actions, it does seem to be a simple matter of deciding what to do and proceeding to do it. When we pay a shopkeeper for what we have bought from him there is no need for any agony of moral decision or for any conscious recapitulation of the christian view of the legitimate grounds for the exchange of material property. A simple purchase is an example of knowing what ought to be done and doing it without more ado. In these simpler cases where there is no evident moral struggle about what ought to be done or about doing our duty, the autonomy of the moral agent appears to be an obvious fact. But there are other areas of moral experience in which this autonomy is much less evident. There is the well-known experience of knowing what we ought to do and finding ourselves unable to do it or of knowing what we ought not to do and being unable to resist the temptation. In such sad circumstances, we discover that we have lost our autonomy without entirely losing our sense of being in some way responsible for our moral weakness. This is, I believe, one of the common facts of human experience which is not fully faced by those who emphasise solely the autonomy of man in making moral decisions. It constitutes a genuine problem which is not solved by concentrating our attention upon the simpler cases where we seem to be quite free and able to act as we will. This absence of autonomy is not explained by devoting our whole attention to those cases where it is present. Another series of grave problems arises about the way in which moral failure may be overcome. It is a fact of experience that many people who have lapsed into some moral failure have later recovered their moral strength. They have undoubtedly fallen but they have also indubitably risen. Their evil will has become a good will. This transition is a mystery. It is no simple autonomous act, because an evil will is not changed into a good will by an act of the evil will. There is a discontinuity between the old life and the new without an interruption in the self-consciousness of the person who has rejected what is evil and turned towards what is good.

An unhealthy will cannot by its own act become a healthy will. This is a genuine problem which is not removed by saying that it is just an illustration of the autonomy of the moral agent. The whole process of repentance and forgiveness, even when we are not thinking of divine forgiveness, discloses problems which are not solved by any simple reference to the autonomy of the moral agent in the presence of the autonomous moral standard. There are depths of human experience here which are not apprehended by any simple moralism.

My purpose in this lecture has been to examine some of the ways in which moral standards and moral agents may be said to be autonomous and to suggest that an acceptance of their autonomy leaves many serious problems unsolved. I began by claiming that the basic use of the word was to describe the ability and freedom of a personal agent to make his own laws. He was autonomous in the sense that he was the author of the laws under which he chose to live. He was not subject to any alien law and he could always revise his own legislation. I then looked more closely at this activity of law-making and distinguished, without separating, the intricate operations of establishing a standard in the form of a law, in selecting a particular legal form of expression and in applying what was thus expressed or in finding that it applied to those who made the application. When autonomy was understood in this way it was plainly somewhat misleading to say that any impersonal standard was autonomous. In itself it possessed no capacity to establish, or express, or apply itself. And, though the moral agent might enjoy a measure of autonomy, it had no meaning apart from any actual situation in which it could be exercised. The actuality of any situation included what was the case about himself and his world, and one feature of this situation was what he assumed to be the case about himself and his world. Even so, as a matter of customary word usage, those who described the moral standard as autonomous meant that it had something of the character of a law which no human will could set aside. The witnesses of wanton cruelty immediately condemned it as if it were against some kind of law. In the moment of making this condemnation, it did not appear to me to be necessary to make any reference to theological beliefs. The need to do so began to show itself when we were seeking to understand the moral standard which did justice to its paradoxical characteristics. Its autonomy was not explained by being affirmed. Moreover, though the autonomy of the moral agent was generally accepted in matters of routine moral decisions, there were other cases in which the moral agent found himself curiously unable to exercise the moral freedom which appeared essential in a responsible moral act. And an array of problems faced us in any attempt to understand the way in which an evil will could change or be changed into a good will. This was no simple act of moral autonomy. In other words, my contention is that though there is a great deal of truth in what is affirmed by those who believe in the autonomy of ethics, there are other ranges and depths of the truth which remain to be explored. If this be so, there is some point in proceeding in the later lectures to investigate the claim that christian theological ethics may offer an interpretation of our moral experience which is truer to experience without being unjust to what is true in secular ethics.

LECTURE 5

THEOLOGICAL ETHICS:
THE CREATIVE WILL OF GOD

The curious characteristics of the moral standard as autonomous and at once other than and authoritatively present in its expressions and applications remains unexplained. It has not been possible to understand the character of the moral standard in terms drawn from our experience of physical standards and personal standards.

The way therefore remains open of trying to interpret it in the terms of traditional christian theism.

There are decisive objections to any interpretation of the moral standard in terms of a crudely anthropomorphic theology. Bad theology leads to bad theological ethics.

Better justice is done to the paradoxical characteristics of the moral standard when it is interpreted as the creative will of God.

The unity in diversity of its expressions and applications is interpreted as bearing some analogy to the unity in diversity of the expressions and applications of a human will.

Its odd status as being at once other than and authoritatively relevant to the actual state of the world is interpreted as being characteristic of the relationship of the creative will of God to the created world which we very imperfectly conceive by analogy from our experience of human creativity.

Its autonomy is not rejected but affirmed when various mistaken views of autonomy have been discarded. It is interpreted as being the creative will of God which wills nothing which is contrary to the true being of any creature. It is acknowledged as being in itself sovereign and unalterable by any human will. It permits and promotes in man genuine progress in its modes of expression and application.

THEOLOGICAL ETHICS:
THE CREATIVE WILL OF GOD

I often think that philosophical writings are very like those ornamental fountains which are to be seen in the extensive grounds of royal palaces. The argument rises for a period as firmly and powerfully as the jet of water rises from its base but a point is reached when the rising waters falter and fall back as broken spray into the pool from which they originally rose. I think that my inquiries are now reaching just such a point, but it might appear rather craven to turn off the water by not delivering the last two lectures in the series.

We have been concerned with the tension between christian theological ethics and the ethics of secular humanism. My contention is that the ethics of christian theology do justice to the manifold features of our moral experience without ignoring what is true in secular ethics. My particular concern has been with the objections to theological ethics which are based upon plain moral grounds. I have not been treating the criticisms which arise from straightforward atheism. I said that in my opinion the basic issue is about the autonomy of ethics, in the sense that the autonomy of the moral standard and the autonomy of the moral agent are taken not only not to need any theological support but to exclude on moral grounds any such assistance. On this view, all theological convictions appear to be morally dispensable. They may be found useful to some people but they ought to be seen to be morally irrelevant by those of greater moral maturity and deeper moral insight. I spent, therefore, three lectures examining the ways in which we think and speak about standards and in analysing the various ways in which autonomy might be understood. I spoke of the perpetual risk of being misled by the terminology which we were using and I drew attention to some of the many paradoxical features of the moral standard. It was admittedly possible in moments of overwhelming moral experience to feel that there was no need for any conscious reference to metaphysics whether theistic or atheistic. It was in the cool hours of reflection that we seemed to be compelled to attribute to the moral standard a series of not easily compatible qualities. It was meaningless as a standard if taken in complete isolation from any actual world for which it served as a standard. But it did not become easily intelligible by being contemplated in relation to the actual world. We were apt to make the mistake of thinking that its nature and operation were just like those of physical and personal standards. It was not easy to understand how the moral standard was related to its expressions and applications. The autonomy of the moral standard was a mystery which was not solved by saying that it was autonomous. It is in the absence of any satisfactory interpretation of this autonomy that I now turn to look afresh at its interpretation in terms of christian theology. Today, therefore, I shall explore the claim that the moral standard may be best understood as the creative will of God. It is, of course, rather awkward to think of the creative will of God apart from his saving will but it is simpler to treat them separately.

Before I commend to you what I believe to be certain positive advantages in a theological interpretation[1] of the moral standard, I must consider one of the most serious objections which I mentioned in my first lecture. This is based upon the distinction between judging what is the case and judging what ought to be the case. It appears, for example, to be a matter of moral common sense that there is an irreducible distinction between saying that an act of wanton cruelty has taken place and judging that it ought not to have taken place. The first judgement appears to be purely factual and the second purely moral. There seems to be no morally justifiable transition from the one to the other. The conclusion is drawn that the moral standard as a statement of what ought to be the case can be seen to be quite different from any information about what is the case in the world to which it refers. The standard in itself seems to stand apart from what is judged to be the case about God, the world, and man. The result is that theological beliefs when taken to be statements of fact are felt to be morally irrelevant and morally repugnant when they claim to be relevant.

There is undoubtedly a distinction in our experience between making a judgement about what is the case and about what ought to be the case. We sense the evident difference between saying that St Francis of Assisi actually lived as a man and saying that he was a good man. The two types of judgement may be made concurrently but they are logically distinguishable. But we must draw a distinction

[1] Cf. C. H. Dodd, *Gospel and Law* (1951); T. W. Manson, *Ethics and the Gospel* (1960); J. Knox, *The Ethic of Jesus in the Teaching of the Church* (1962).

between recognising this logical distinction and the separate question whether it is a purely logical matter. It may be possible to appreciate the distinction without at the same time thinking of any actual world to which it may apply. The purely logical enterprise may be practicable. But once we are making the distinction in reference to some actual world, we are bound to have some conception of the actual world in which the distinction is being made. In this case, those who make judgements as to what is the case always have some opinion about the sense in which they and their world are in being. They have some view both of what it means to be in being and of what is taken to be in being. There is some content in what they take to be the case. Moreover, what they take to be the case may correspond or fail to correspond with what in fact is the case. They may be right or they may be wrong about what is the case. These are not logical but ontological questions. They may be ignored by the logician but they cannot be overlooked by the metaphysician. The question whether one type of judgement may with logical propriety be drawn from another type of judgement is not the same as the problem of the relation of being and value in whatever is taken to be the case about the actual world. To distinguish between a factual and a moral judgement about St Francis takes us very little way towards a solution of the mysterious union of being and value in his personality.

The phrase 'what is the case' is open to a wide variety of interpretations. It may be taken to mean the conception of whatever is in being. This includes whatever is in being in any sense which is distinguishable from not being in being. It is the class of what is in being without any attempt to say what things are in being or whether there are various types of things which are in being. It is a blank totality. When we direct our attention towards what is in fact the case about some actual world, we inevitably begin to have some notion of the kind of thing which we take to be in being. We are thinking of something which is the case. Now, I suspect that in thinking of what is actually the case, we are inclined to think primarily of some state of physical things which is the case. I believe that we are biased towards the belief that what is the case refers to situations which are composed of impersonal entities. It is possible that the actual cases which we most easily apprehend are cases of physical being. In speaking of a case, our predecessors may have been predisposed towards an interest in physical situations by calling such a situation a 'case'. What was the situation originally described as a 'case'? I believe that the word originally described one of the possible ways in which something fell which was capable of falling. If, for example, I balanced a pencil upright on this desk and then allowed it to fall over, it would fall in some definite direction and remain at rest where it had fallen. In such a case, what is to count as the case? Ought I to have in mind the whole natural order in which this trivial incident occurs? Should I concentrate my attention upon the pencil as it falls? Am I primarily interested in the fact that its falling was arrested by the flat top of the desk? Am I most concerned that it has fallen where it has fallen? Should I call it a case if the pencil was falling perpetually into a bottomless pit, or should I in that case say that the case is not closed? In any case, I am taking the case to consist of the observable physical movements and states attained after the movements have been completed. In so far as I allow my thinking about what is the case to be affected by such antecedent experiences, I am likely to assume that impersonal being must be the essence of what is the case. I am biased towards some kind of impersonal interpretation of being. Whatever may be the reason for having a propensity towards the interpretation of what is the case in impersonal terms, I see no good reason why we should follow this practice. Our primary experience is of personal being. We have a closer acquaintance with being persons than with being anything else. The fundamental problem is that we are still quite unable to think adequately of what we know ourselves to be. There are many aspects of our being which are not effectively caught in the web of our thinking. The enterprise is somewhat like trying to carry sunlight in a string bag. But I believe we are rather better at recognising ways of thinking about ourselves which can be seen to be inadequate. Amongst these evidently inadequate efforts is the endeavour to think of personal being in impersonal terms. We are on the wrong road if we assume that what is the case about a personal being must be just like what is the case about a being which is impersonal. The two cases differ essentially. It is far easier to say what is so about the impersonal than about the personal. The whole truth about a person is not given when a report is presented of his observable movements or when a list is provided of what he had consciously in mind at a particular time. What is the case about him includes both his being a person and the particular personal state in which he happens to be. The deeper truth about his being is still unnoticed if his present state is taken to be no more than one which might just have been a different state. If there was any truth in my earlier contention that he is failing to be a person when he ignores or flouts the standards of his own being; if it be admitted that his being as a person involves his relation to the moral standard, it is simply not the case that he is a person to whom in some ramshackle way the moral standard ought to be attached. It is the case that he is a moral being who may or may not be living an actual moral life. To identify a person with his words, thoughts and deeds is to mistake his being and to take an impoverished view of what is the case about him. No one who wishes to be called an empiricist ought to insist that what is the case is not open to any interpretation which is other than impersonal. To do so would be to lose his being as an empiricist.

In our experience of the manifold character of personal being, I think we may have some slight insight into the character of ultimate being. In our own case, there is always a discrepancy between what we actually are and what we ought to be. And we have also some sense of a discrepancy between our actual apprehension of what we ought to be and what in truth we ought to be. The perfection of our being is beyond our full understanding and beyond our powers of execution. I believe we can dimly conceive that this kind of discrepancy must be absent in God. In Him what is the case and what ought to be the case are the same. There is no disheartening margin between the two. In such a case there is no necessity for an awkward transition from what is the case to what ought to be the case. Where there is no distance to travel, there is no need to undertake the journey. But we must not speak too glibly here. God is not a case of an impersonal being which is larger than those known to us nor is he a case of a human being who happens to be in various ways larger than we are. God is unique. In thinking of him in personal analogies we are always straining our language to breaking point and we shall not all agree about the point at which the break occurs. I am bound to confess that when I reach the point of speaking about God, I would much prefer to remain silent. But I am quite sure that we cannot dismiss the possibility of theological ethics by making unqualified assertions about an absolute ontological distinction between what is the case and what ought to be the case.

A particular instance of the objection based upon the distinction between what is the case and what ought to be the case is the misgiving which is often expressed about interpreting the moral standard as the will of God. This criticism is often associated with a very understandable hesitation in speaking of God in personal terms. There are undeniable problems about thinking of God in terms drawn from our experience of the structure and working of human personality even when these terms are used analogically. To believe that their use is ultimately unavoidable is very different from thinking that no problems arise in their use. These difficulties deserve serious study but here I am confining my attention to those objections which have a plain moral basis. The moral objection to any interpretation of the moral standard as the will of God is that there appears to be no legitimate transition from the knowledge that something is willed by God to the knowledge that what is willed is good. From the judgement of fact there seems to be no logically proper movement to the moral judgement. If what is willed by God is taken for that reason alone to be good, there is a deep-seated fear that the moral standard is no more than what God happened to will for no good reason whatever. In a sense the formal autonomy of the moral standard is maintained but its moral dignity is lost. And if what is willed by God is good because it is in accord with the moral standard to which he is subject, it appears that the standard in itself lies beyond any theological interpretation. God cannot be the explanation of what has authority over him. These puzzles have been perennial. They occur when we assume that the will of God is like a human will which is not good or evil solely in virtue of being willed. It is a commonplace of moral experience that, for example, no command is morally good or evil simply because it is commanded. What is willed or commanded is judged to be good or evil by reference to the moral standard. But it is a mistake to treat the will of God as though it was just like a human will. It is an error to think of God as a finite person in the company of other finite persons inhabiting a common world including an autonomous moral standard. Even so, to discard a crude theology is only a step towards a more delicate interpretation of the being and activity of God. An act of pure creation is beyond our experience. We have no clear and distinct idea of the creative will of God. In our speaking of God as creative, we cannot eliminate every element of mystery from the language which we use. Some may say that in that case all our language about God is becoming so qualified that it virtually loses all meaning. It has been said that theological language is gradually losing its life by the imposition of a thousand cuts. But if we chose to

99

argue by opposing one illustration to another, we might reply that each qualification made by a careful philosophical theologian is more like the minute cuts made by a patient wood-carver who is gradually transforming the natural shape of a piece of wood into a work of art. The important point is not the polemical exchanges of illustrations but whether, having progressed beyond a crude understanding of the moral standard as the will of God, we can advance towards an understanding of the creative will of God which we can use with a measure of confidence.

I have tried to show that both forms of the above objection to any interpretation of the autonomous moral standard as the will of God are based upon a mistake about what is the case about God. Mistaken views of God cannot provide satisfactory theological ethics. Bad theology leads to bad ethics. When belief in God is taken to be belief about the character of ultimate being, it is not the case that what is ultimate must inevitably be interpreted in impersonal terms and expressed in analogies drawn from our experience of what is the case in physical situations. God is not a thing. And it is not the case that, if we interpret ultimate being in personal terms, we are bound to think of God as just like a human person living in a human environment. God is not a larger human person. When these two mistakes are made it is not at all surprising that theological ethics appear to be incompatible with any belief in the autonomy of the moral standard. It is neither identical with nor somehow based upon either a thing or a finite personal will. To follow either of these two roads is not to oppose christian theological ethics but to walk away from them.

Though I know of no interpretation of the autonomy of the moral standard which is free from obscurities and difficulties, I believe that we are least unsuccessful if we interpret it as the creative will of God. I think that this way of understanding it does not destroy its autonomy and throws some light upon its curious relevance to the situations in which it stands autonomous over both its expressions and its applications. A satisfactory understanding of the moral standard must not be offensive to our everyday moral experience and must in some measure satisfy the legitimate questions which occur to us when we reflect upon our experience.

We noticed in the last lecture that the moral standard was not autonomous in the strict sense of being able and free to make its own laws. The adjective was used analogically to affirm that the moral standard was not morally subordinate to any standard other than itself. It had moral authority for its own sake and in its own right. It possessed moral sovereignty. Now, I see no good reason why this kind of moral autonomy should be undermined by a theological interpretation of the moral standard which avoids the mistakes of assuming that ultimate reality is impersonal or that God is just like a human person. Let us explore the probable effects of interpreting the moral standard as the creative will of God. I realise, of course, that many of my contemporaries do not believe in God and that, if they do believe in God, they may hesitate to think of him as the creator of the world, but at the present moment I am seeking to expound and defend an interpretation of the autonomy of the moral standard as understood by those who believe in God as the creator of the world. I am making this exploration as a christian believer in God accepted as the one on whom the world depends. I do not see how this belief rightly understood need reduce the autonomy of the moral standard. Our immediate experience of an obligation which we accept as binding need not be weakened when it is interpreted as an experience of the creative will of God working within us. In this case we are not thinking that the moral standard is somehow subordinated to the creative will. It is an expression of that will. To think of the moral standard is to think of the creative will of God. We are thinking of one thing in two ways. It is really pointless to ask whether the standard is subordinate to the creative will or the creative will to the standard because nothing is superior or inferior to itself. And when the moral standard is interpreted in this way it seems to me that its autonomy is not disparaged but affirmed in the most definite way possible. As the creative will of God it is in no way subject to the will of man. No human decision can abrogate or modify what is the case about the will of God as our creator. The autonomy of the moral standard is here not simply affirmed without explanation but interpreted as a characteristic of what is ultimately the case. Moreover, the creative will of God is accepted as autonomous in the sense that He is not subordinate to any authority greater than his own. His autonomous will is understood as being not only authoritative over the wills of men but over all principalities and powers which may in some way exist apart from God. His will is morally sovereign over whatever exists. I cannot see how the autonomy of the moral standard can be taken more seriously than it is taken in theological ethics when care is taken to avoid an implied atheism on the one hand and a crudely anthropomorphic theology on the other.

I have been suggesting to you that the autonomy of the moral standard is nowhere more adequately affirmed than in theological ethics when these are rightly understood. When the moral standard is interpreted as the creative will of God it is not open to many of the legitimate criticisms which may be made of cruder forms of theological ethics. But we must proceed to glance at some of the more positive advantages of a theological interpretation of our moral experience. I think, for instance, that to interpret the moral standard as the creative will of God goes some way towards an elucidation of the curious ambiguity which is characteristic of the moral status of expressions of the moral standard. They retain and lose their moral adequacy in a quite bewildering way. They are the chameleons of the moral linguistic universe. There is a whole range of expressions from most particular precepts to most general principles and laws. All are useful but they are not all equally useful in all situations. All in some sense embody the moral standard but in every case the standard itself is neither wholly identical with its expression nor wholly other than the form in which it is expressed. It is at once transcendent and immanent in regard to its expressions. The problem is to find a way of thinking about the moral standard in relation to its expressions which neither removes it to a limbo of meaninglessness nor annihilates it by identifying it with one or other of its expressions. Our understanding of this baffling relationship has been impeded by the unfortunate habit of describing it in terms of the physical analogy of expression. This has been unfortunate in two ways. We have tended to assume that the act of expressing the moral standard is comparable to that of imposing by pressure a new physical form upon some kind of plastic material. This analogy is not illuminating. It is inept. We might realise its inappropriateness more vividly if we substituted the habit of referring to the variety of compressions of the moral standard. The use of this physical analogy has also been unfortunate in encouraging the conclusion that the moral standard is related to all its expressions in the same way. A qualitative diversity of analogies should have suggested a diversity in the relationship. In fact, we have already noticed an important distinction between an expression adapted to a single situation and an expression in the form of a rule or principle adapted to a series of comparable situations. It became plain that the moral standard in itself was expressed in a diversity of forms which were appropriate for use in a diversity of situations. I suggested that the moral agent, being unable to comprehend the moral standard in itself habitually apprehended it under a diversity of expressed forms which could be accepted as a guide to moral conduct. It seemed simplest to interpret this operation in terms of a human will which is present in its expressions without being identical with any of them. We have daily experience of the outcome of this operation without, I believe, being able to understand how it takes place. We do not observe the transition from silence to speech. We simply find that we have spoken. We have experience of our wills being incorporated in expressions without becoming identified with them. Our wills are at once outside and inside their expressions. I hope I realise how hazardous it is to think of the creative will of God by analogy from our own willing, but I can see no less inadequate way of interpreting the ambiguous moral status of expressions of the moral standard than to say that they are related to the moral standard in itself in a manner comparable to the way in which a human will is related to its various forms of expression. This manner of interpretation does some justice to the curious way in which the moral standard is neither the same as its expressions nor utterly unrelated to them. It may, at least, be claimed that this delicate problem which is not elucidated by a simple affirmation of the autonomy of the moral standard is faced by theological ethics.

A further problem which is not answered by a constant reiteration of belief in the autonomy of the moral standard is its applicability to the actual world in which we find ourselves. I am not here thinking of the ways in which a moral agent may apply the moral standard to his conduct in the world but of the ways in which this standard applies to the world. This is not an act of application but a state of applying. When we think of the moral standard as applying to the world we may be thinking of the curious fact that it has the characteristic of being relevant to human situations or we may be thinking of the mysterious way in which it is morally authoritative in human situations. It would have no moral authority if it were totally irrelevant and as a proposed course of action it might be relevant and practicable without being morally obligatory. The applicability touches both what is the case and what ought to be the case. The problem of the way in which the moral standard holds on to or holds in the world is not ignored by theological ethics.

It is far easier to say that this problem of the applicability of the moral standard must not be ignored than to offer any solution, but I believe that a theological interpretation of this applicability is still worth serious consideration. The difficulty is to find a way of thinking satisfactorily of the manner in which the moral standard holds, or grips, or clasps, or clutches the actual situations to which it applies. It is quite obvious that these words are quite liable to be misleading in that they describe the ways in which we may use our hands to grasp a physical object. Something is held, or gripped, or clasped. As the moral standard has no physical hands and as the human situations are more complex than physical things, we cannot use such language literally. And, as we saw earlier, we are misled if we think that the moral standard applies to the world as a yardstick may be taken and placed alongside the physical material which is being measured. The yardstick and the material have no essential need to be side by side and neither has any obligation to be longer or shorter than it is. All the physical analogies are misleading. The moral standard is simply not applicable as insulating tape is applicable to an electric cable. And we may also be misled by the use of one type of rather inept analogy into the precipitate belief that the moral standard must always be related to the actual world in the same way. In view of the diversity of the components of the actual world of our experience, we may well be disposed to expect a diversity of relationships which may be overlooked by employing only one kind of analogy. For example, the distinction which appears to exist between personal and impersonal beings is not easy to eliminate and, if it be accepted, we are bound to expect that the relation of these very different types of being to the moral standard will be different. It is unlikely that the autonomous moral standard will be found to hold of each in exactly the same way. I suggested earlier that a personal being was a being with personal standards. These were not applied to him as a bandage might be applied to his wrist. They were the standards of his being. Apart from these standards he was not a personal being. In obedience to them he displayed and explored what it meant to be a person. He was most truly himself in accepting them.

I still think that if we advance beyond the bare acknowledgement that the moral standard applies to us and seek some way of understanding how this application occurs, we may usefully interpret the moral standard as the presence of the creative and sustaining will of God. We have, of course, no direct experience of the creative will of God. We are not creators. But we do have experience of being the authors of the works of our hands and minds. We are authorities about our own works in the sense that we know the creative intention from which they sprang and the creative work which was involved. This may give us some analogical insight into the will of God as creator and we may interpret personal being as a creation of God. This interpretation is immediately confused if we forget the complexity of what is the case about being a person. It is not only the case that a person is in the actual state in which he is at any particular time but it is also the case that his being essentially includes the personal standards in which he finds his true fulfilment. In dutiful submission to them, he may be said to be living in obedience to the will of his creator. This is not submission to an alien tyranny nor is it a capricious exercise of an irresponsible autonomy. It is a matter of being himself. Precisely for this reason, the creative will of God as it is more fully understood is found to be in accord with his reason and his conscience. It is simply a mistake to expect the creative will of God to show its presence by being very different from our finest moral insights. The process of discovering the creative will of God for the personal beings which He has created should be continuous. Its presence within us should provide a progressive assurance about many of our moral convictions and should place under constant scrutiny the moral traditions which we receive. It ought to be the source of moral progress and should be a resolute enemy of the hideous fanaticisms which would extinguish the light of reason in matters of human conduct. Moreover, the moral standard which applies to personal beings must apply to them in the world which they inhabit. It is unsatisfying to affirm that the moral standard for man is autonomous and to say nothing of its relation to the natural environment in which he lives. If the natural order is not in some way explained as being related to the autonomous moral order, they are left standing side by side in unexplained juxtaposition. If it be said that it is meaningless to ask for a reason for the natural order, we are left with a given situation to which the moral standard is relevant for no intelligible reason. The natural world is treated as a stage on which the moral play takes place without any inquiry about the relation which makes the play a physical possibility or about one play being better than another. If the natural world is taken to mean the physical world in which man emerged as a moral being, the origin of the autonomous moral standard remains obscure. He appears to be a resident alien in a world in which he is not at home. A full understanding of the moral standard as applicable in our actual world must include some study of the curious fact that it is found to apply. In the traditional christian beliefs about God as the creator of the world, the affirmation is made that God is the single source of what we distinguish into the natural order and the moral order. What we call the two orders are related from the beginning in that God is the author of both of them. They do not have to be introduced to one another as though they had never met. I do not believe for a moment that a theological interpretation of the applicability of the moral standard to the personal and the impersonal world leaves no problems unsolved. But I would claim that this problem is not solved by being left unanswered and that a not unreasonable answer is offered in the tradition of christian theological ethics.

In this lecture I have been offering some defence of christian theological ethics. Many important issues have been omitted. I began by claiming that the distinction between what is the case and what ought to be the case is meaningless until those who rely upon the distinction are more explicit about their conception of what constitutes a case and about the type of being possessed by the components of a case. What is the case about impersonal being is simply not what is the case about personal being. I then contended that those who rejected any interpretation of the moral standard as the will of God often did so on the unconscious basis of a very crude theology. They seemed at times to be victims of the gross theological anthropomorphism which at other times they condemned. Outlining the more positive advantages of theological ethics, I suggested that they safeguarded the autonomy of the moral standard in a manner which did not morally deny it and I put forward the claim that the problems about the expressions and applications of the moral standard were more squarely faced in theological ethics than was sometimes the case in ethics which did not go beyond affirming the autonomy of the moral standard. At several points in this lecture, some of the rabbits have been emerging which I may have appeared to be placing in the hat at an earlier stage. The really serious question is whether I put them in the hat or whether an unprejudiced investigation shows that they were already in the hat when I received it, so that I am truly finding what I have not myself inserted.

LECTURE 6

THEOLOGICAL ETHICS: THE SAVING WILL OF GOD

When the moral standard is interpreted as the saving will of God, the divine will is being interpreted as at once creative and saving.

There are real moral problems in reconciling belief in the autonomy of the moral agent and belief in the saving will of God. And the reward of eternal life can be represented in a morally distasteful way.

But belief in the autonomy of the moral agent is also hard to reconcile with the fact of moral failure and moral progress.

These problems are reduced, though they are not fully solved, when the moral standard is interpreted, within the whole system of christian doctrine, as being the divine will which both establishes the standard and wills to save those who fail to observe it.

The claim is made that christian theological ethics do justice to what is true in the moral insights of secular humanism and provide a fuller interpretation of the whole range of our experience of living and failing to live in accord with the moral standard.

THEOLOGICAL ETHICS:
THE SAVING WILL OF GOD

In the last lecture I sought to show that the autonomy of the moral standard was not denied but affirmed in theological ethics when these were rightly understood. I suggested that objections based upon the distinction between what is the case and what ought to be the case were always lacking in precision when this distinction was only stated and not explained. There are many ways of interpreting whatever is said to be the case. When a case is taken to be an instance of a number of possible cases, a full statement of the case would include information about the conditions which make a plurality of cases possible. And what is taken to be a case is *as known to an observer* always a selection of interesting facts which are distinguished from those that are found to be of no interest. When what is the case is taken to be the selection of facts which are open to sensible observation, the conclusion is inevitable that what ought to be the case has no foundation in fact. The decision has already been taken that the real facts are the sensible facts. It is not surprising that on this view there is no ultimate place for theological ethics. But, actually, it is both possible and permissible to take the view that personal being is not reducible to what is impersonal. It can be affirmed that it is the case that personal being is primary. On this view, it is not surprising that the moral standard should be interpreted as the will of God. The assertion is then made that the autonomous moral standard is the will of God. This is open to justifiable criticism when it is assumed that the will of God is just like the will of a human person. The autonomy of the moral standard cannot be defended when God is interpreted as though he were just like a human being who is subject to the moral law. These objections do not, I suggested, exclude the interpretation of the moral standard as the will of God accepted as creator of the world. The creative will of God must always remain mysterious to us as we have no experience of absolute creation, but I think it offers some light on two problems which cannot be ignored by any theory of the autonomy of the moral standard which advances beyond the simple assertion that it is autonomous. It gives us some insight into the curious relationship between the standard and its manifold expressions which are neither identical with the standard nor wholly unrelated to it. And it provides a reasonable solution to the problem of the way in which an autonomous moral standard can be found to apply both to personal beings and to the world in which they find themselves. When a moral standard is accepted as autonomous over the human inhabitants of the actual world, the problem cannot be evaded of seeking to understand why the natural world permits or promotes the operation of an autonomous standard. I did not, and I could not, claim that the interpretation of the autonomous moral standard as the creative will of God left no problems unsolved but I do think that, rightly understood, it is not open to some of the popular objections and I think it offers some answer to inescapable problems which are sometimes neglected.

In this lecture, I shall try to show that the autonomous

moral standard should be interpreted as the saving will of God. I am not suggesting that God has two wills. God is at once creator and saviour. His will is both creative and saving. As in the last lecture I shall endeavour to show that this interpretation rightly understood is not open to some of the objections which are popularly made against it and that it also meets in part certain problems which are more easily overlooked than answered. As usual, I shall be giving my primary attention to the objections and problems which have a predominantly moral character. I am afraid that in a single lecture my treatment of many serious issues must be very superficial but I came to the conclusion that it was legitimate and useful in our present situation to undertake a wider survey which might help to place in perspective other acts of microscopic analysis. We can become so engrossed in minute conceptual or verbal analysis that we forget what has not been included in our immediate field of view and consequently reach conclusions that are lacking in balance. I would be very happy to see the christian interpretation of life as the supreme manifestation of common sense.

I think that the conscientious secular moralist may honestly say that his major misgiving about a theological interpretation of the moral standard is not the claim that it may be interpreted as the creative will of God. While not himself accepting this claim, he may agree that it may be true. He is likely to be far less willing to entertain the possibility that the moral standard may be the will of God understood as at once creative and saving. To speak of saving will is uncongenial to him. I believe that his misgiving arises from two main causes. A confident believer in the autonomy of the moral agent is sure that such an agent knows the autonomous moral standard and is free to obey it or to disobey it. To possess moral freedom implies that the agent is free to act without assistance from God or from other men. His being autonomous consists in not being dependent upon receiving help from others. The moral worth of his willing and acting depends upon his being the genuine author of his acts. He is praiseworthy or blameworthy precisely because he is an autonomous agent. His autonomy is therefore infringed if anything is taken to be his own activity which in truth is due to the activity of others. This is the first main cause of misgiving about accepting belief in the saving will of God. On this view, the autonomous agent does not need the help of divine grace and it would be immoral for this grace to be offered or accepted. Each person must be left to fight his own moral battles. As moral agents we are essentially alone and we ought to be left alone. In moments of moral confidence we think that we have no need of any saving will other than our own, and in moments of moral diffidence we know that we ought not to accept any help from an external saving will and that it would be morally wrong for any such help to be offered to us. There are still more obvious objections to any suggestion that the grace of God is an irresistible power which overwhelms the autonomy of the moral agent. Until these misgivings are removed or reduced, there is no genuine desire or readiness to interpret the creative will of God as a will which is seeking to save the world.

The conscientious secular humanist has a second ground for misgiving. This is when the saving will of God is represented as offering some hope of survival after death. Christians may become so accustomed to this hope that it may need a little thought and imagination to realise that many morally serious people may feel indifferent about this hope and therefore lack serious interest in the claim that it is the purpose of God to save us from annihilation. A number of moral considerations are often sustaining this indifference. It looks so simple to accept death as a natural fact and to rejoice in the confidence that this fact of nature cannot overthrow the autonomy of the moral standard. The martyr for the truth is upheld by the conviction that the truth will survive his own death. And at the level of ordinary acts of honesty and kindliness, there seems to be no obvious necessity to make any explicit reference to the fact that we are all subject to death. And there is the perennial moral objection that what is right ought not to be done in order to obtain the reward of life after death. It looks as though duty is being done for the sake of self-interest. And a preoccupation with the attainment of eternal life may also be morally offensive when it leads to a quite excessive indifference to the affairs of this life. Thus, for a variety of reasons, there can often be an absence of authentic concern about the possibility of a saving divine will which may offer the hope of everlasting life.

I believe that there is some truth in these misgivings but I do not think that they are based upon an adequate study of our moral experience and I doubt whether they are decisive against a trust in the saving will of God when this is properly understood. When we are thinking of the autonomy of anything, we tend to think of it as possessing or exercising its autonomy. Our attention is focused upon the autonomy as our attention may be concentrated upon the buoyancy of a balloon. In such a case, we envisage the balloon as floating in the air. We do not envisage it on the ground when it has lost its buoyancy. The very use of the word autonomy or buoyancy inclines us to ignore the situations in which the autonomy is for some reason not exercised and the occasions when the buoyancy has disappeared. I think that we may make a similar mistake in thinking about the autonomy of the moral agent. Undoubtedly there are many occasions when he appears to be in full possession of his moral autonomy. But there are many other occasions when the exercise of this autonomy is seriously impeded. If we consult our own moral experience, I believe that we can recollect many situations in which we have been at a loss about what we ought to do, and other cases in which we have known what we ought to do and have not had the moral power to do it. Moreover, sometimes when we have been conscious of some aspect of our duty, we have seen later that we took an unduly narrow view of what it was. We did not possess the autonomous power either of discovering our whole duty or of fulfilling it. It is very probably true to say that confidence in the autonomy of the individual moral agent has receded considerably during the last fifty years. Liberal optimism has been losing ground to the more pessimistic view that the individual has little or no power to resist or control his circumstances. It is increasingly believed that human personality is shaped by the environment in which it develops. This has often led to the conclusion that we are not responsible for what we become. My point here is not to examine our experience of the innumerable occasions on which our moral autonomy seems to be absent or in very poor working order but to claim that these depressing facts of human experience ought not to be ignored by those who proclaim the autonomy of the moral agent. The facts of moral weakness and moral failure constitute problems for those who affirm that the moral agent is autonomous. They are not morally trivial or irrelevant facts of the situation. Whoever asserts that man is morally autonomous is under an obligation to give some account of the curious fact that men are unable to exercise the autonomy which they are said to possess. Whatever is true in the assertion that the moral agent is autonomous is not denied by the insistence that the problem of his moral frailty should not be passed over in silence. Failure is not eliminated by talking only of success.

This problem of the recurrent inability of the moral agent to act autonomously is not ignored in the tradition of theological ethics. The doctrine of the Fall of Man is an attempt to account for the moral weakness and moral failure which are constant facts of our human experience. I am not here concerned to offer a defence of any traditional or more recent solutions to the problem of moral evil. I would be bound to confess that I know of no explanation of the presence of moral wickedness in human history which offers complete moral satisfaction. My claim is not that the problem of evil is solved in christian theology but that it is not overlooked. It is recognised as a problem and some attempt is made to give an answer. It is important to realise that the answer which is given springs from the whole of christian doctrine and not from a single doctrine taken in isolation. The doctrines of christianity form a certain system or economy. The capacity of the system as a whole to interpret the facts of human experience and history is not displayed when a single doctrine is examined without reference to the others. If the scheme of christian doctrine is not presented as a whole, the impression may be given that when reference to one doctrine fails to be convincing a despairing appeal is made to a doctrine which would otherwise not have been mentioned. This is misleading. Any defence of christian theological ethics must be made upon the basis of the whole system of christian doctrine.

It is possible to be persuaded that moral weakness and failure constitute a genuine moral problem and to admit that a saving will of God would be relevant to these problems without at the same time admitting that there is any moral necessity to believe in a saving will of God which is able to save us from eternal death. As long as annihilating mortality is not seen as making any difference to the moral life, it is unlikely that there will be a serious interest in the possibility that eternal life may be available through the power of God. Until this outlook is changed, the moral agent is likely to lack interest in the possibility of being saved from annihilating death and he may often feel that any such interest is morally regrettable or even offensive. Great care is needed in giving an answer which does not deepen the misgivings which it was intended to assuage. The main problem is the moral relevance of annihilating mortality to the autonomy of the moral standard. I have already admitted that I think many of the simpler moral duties can be seen to be binding upon us without any conscious reference to the existence of God and the hope of survival after death. When a small fire is in danger of spreading and destroying a house, I see no reason why a secular humanist and a devout christian should not work together in extinguishing it without wasting any time in a discussion of the justification of theological ethics. They are better engaged in putting out the fire. The relevance of some hope of life after death becomes more evident when the foreseeable consequences almost certainly include the death of people engaged in the case. There are the martyrs who die for their faith and those who lay down their lives that others may live. In such situations the intricate relationship between the autonomy of the moral standard and the fact of human mortality is more plainly open to inspection. Questions which need not be asked in the simpler cases of morally responsible living press for an answer. Their pressure is felt particularly by those who deliberately or as a matter of habit tend to judge moral issues by the consequences. In fact, they are mistaken if they assume that their decisions are made solely by reference to the anticipated results. No decision would ever be reached if the observer was able to foresee what would happen but unable to judge whether he approved or disapproved of what he foresaw. He requires a standard by which the foreseen consequences may be judged. He does not judge solely by the consequences but by these in reference to his moral standard. But it is also a mistake to forget other factors which have their necessary place in his complex act of making a moral judgement. He must not overlook the fact that all personal consequences require the existence of persons in whom they are actualised. Personal results do not exist apart from persons who exist. If, then, the foreseeable consequences almost certainly include the death of people engaged in the case, the question arises whether any attention ought to be given to the fact that someone is going to be deprived of the opportunity of sharing in the consequences. It is necessary to face the problem whether the person who is likely to lose his life has any claim to be considered when the probable consequences are being assessed. Whether his death is his annihilation or a transition to some kind of life after death is not a matter which can be left for later consideration. It is not a matter of merely future importance. It has immediate relevance. Whether the one who dies will or will not in some sense outlive his death is an important fact in the case. His destiny is part of the actual situation in which the decision is being made. I am not at this stage defending the christian hope of everlasting life but suggesting that, in those cases where someone in the case is likely to lose his life, the question of survival after death has an evident relevance that is not immediately obvious in the course of the simpler moral decisions which involve a short series of obvious temporal consequences. My own belief is that the reference to survival of death is implicit in all moral decisions because, in dealing with people, we cannot avoid having some view of what it means to be a person and I believe that to be capable of surviving death is a characteristic of personal being. To pursue this point here would lead me away from my main contention that belief in the autonomy of the moral standard and of the moral agent does not make the fact of human mortality irrelevant.

But there is a great difference between acknowledging

that the possibility of surviving death cannot be a matter of indifference to those who believe in these autonomies and finding a way of thinking about this possibility which is free from moral objection. The hope of eternal life can be presented in a way which suggests that the reason for obeying the moral standard is for the sake of some remoter consideration. It can appear that dutiful living is being commended for some kind of reward which is other than that found in the fulfilment of duty. Virtue can be recommended as a good investment. But I think we might have in mind that the question whether there is a life after death is not dependent upon the manner in which such a belief is used as a motive for right conduct. Whether anything is a fact is not determined by our attitude towards it. And I do not believe that the hope of eternal life need always be viewed as a crude reward for living in accord with the autonomous moral standard. It is possible to believe that acts which are not done for the sake of reward nevertheless deserves some kind of reward. It is difficult to express this point in a way which is not morally offensive but I think we do realise a distinction between doing what is right for some kind of alien reward and acknowledging that right living is entitled to some kind of recognition. This recognition is in a sense a reward. It is a kind of recompense. Once we begin to admit that some kind of reward is morally congruous, I think that we shall find it hard to be morally satisfied with a recognition of virtuous living which does not include a confidence that the virtuous man is not annihilated at death. The greater our moral admiration, the greater will be our puzzlement or distress at the thought that he in no way survives his death. I find it hard to say that this moral experience yields more than a moral demand for the reality of some kind of eternal life but I see no reason why such a belief should be interpreted as no more than a matter of collecting the wages of virtue. In short, the relation of moral autonomy to human mortality is no simple matter and it deserves a far fuller and deeper treatment than I have just given but I remain convinced that the issue cannot be dismissed by being ignored. Eternal life can be regarded as a fitting fulfilment of the exercise of moral autonomy in obedience to an autonomous moral standard. If these claims are true, there is good reason for the secular humanist to continue taking a serious interest in the christian claim that the moral standard as the creative will of God is also a saving will which can offer the hope of everlasting life.

If I have been able to persuade you that those who believe in the autonomies of the moral life ought to take a serious interest in the question of a divine saving will which may offer victory over moral failure and death, there is good reason for persevering in our inquiry concerning the defence of theological ethics. What I now hope to do is to explore the concept of a saving will of God by examining the features which must characterise a will capable of offering some hope of triumph over moral frailty and human mortality. We may be led to see that only the will of God is capable of fulfilling these demands. My argument will move through two stages. In the first, I shall examine some interpretations of the autonomy of the moral standard which, though partly true, nevertheless fall short of offering any hope of overcoming either our moral frailty or our subjection to annihilating death. In the second stage, I shall consider more positively the reasonableness of interpreting the saving power as the will of God which is both creative and saving.

In considering some of the interpretations of the autonomous moral standard which preclude or do not explicitly include any reference to a saving divine will, we must recall some of the distinctions which I made earlier in my analysis of the ways in which we speak of standards. I suggested that it was a mistake to think of the moral standard as though it was just like the physical replica of what we call a physical standard. If we think of the moral standard in this way we find ourselves thinking of a standard which somehow stands alongside the course of human behaviour without having any intelligible relation to it and without having any moral authority which is explicable. In just standing, it is not an intelligible standard. And, even if it could be interpreted as a relevant and authoritative standard, there is no suggestion that it has any function or purpose beyond being a means of measuring what is measured. Standards understood as replicas have in themselves no moral autonomy. They may be useful as providing various units of measurement but they contain no kind of demand or request that what is measured ought to be, for example, of a certain length. When the moral standard is identified with some expression which is impersonal it offers no kind of assistance or hope to what is not in accord with the expressed standard. It is quite indifferent to what observers might call success or failure. There is clearly a greater possibility of interpreting the moral standard as a saving will if the standard is interpreted in terms of will. An impersonal standard has no prerogative of mercy and forgiveness, whereas these are possible in a personal will. But we must not advance too rapidly. It is possible to think of a will which is intent upon the standards to be achieved without any deep concern about helping people to attain them or much compassion for those who fail. We can imagine the moral standard as an exacting and merciless will devoid of sympathy and understanding. This happens when the moral standard is interpreted in the form of a law. This type of expression permits a high degree of precision in distinguishing what is and what is not in accord with the standard but it contains no hint that the will behind the law may be a compassionate will. Understood purely as a law, the standard has a rigidity which misrepresents the subtlety of the moral standard in itself. But even if the autonomous moral standard is acknowledged to be both within and above the various forms and shapes which it assumes, it is still possible to doubt whether the standard in itself is in any sense a saving will. It is not impossible to think of a creative divine will which is intent upon the achievement of perfection without a generous concern for those who fail to achieve perfection. If this is the sole consideration, the creative will would have no use for those who had failed beyond reasonable hope of recovery. There is undeniably something majestic about a creative will which judges magisterially between moral success and moral failure but such a will offers no hope to those who fail. Even when the pattern of creative development is most sensitively and imaginatively conceived, a distinction remains between willing that this should be achieved and caring for those who find its achievement far beyond their powers. The exquisite insistence upon excellence does not necessarily include a compassionate concern for those whose degree of excellence is less than perfect. Quite obviously, as I have tried to show earlier, we cannot avoid the analogical use of language in speaking and thinking about the autonomous moral standard, but I believe that beyond the curtain of analogies we can realise that there is a distinction between a will which is purely creative and one which is both creative and saving.

There are undoubtedly the most daunting difficulties in conceiving what is meant if it is said that the moral standard is the creative and saving will of God. God is not man. The will of God is not just like the will of man. The creative will of God is not just like our will to make new things out of the available material. The re-creative will of God is not just like our will to repair or make perfect what has lost or failed to attain its proper perfection. The acts which we call creative and re-creative are very different from the analogically comparable acts of God. But I think we ought not to relapse into complete silence. Something of some use may be said. We can begin by ceasing to think in terms of distinguishable wills. We are not compelled to think that there are two autonomous wills which may or may not happen to work together in the same creative and re-creative acts. We do better to think in terms of a person whose will in time is engaged in what we call acts of creation and re-creation. To the agent himself, there need be no inconsistency in these two activities. It is the same person who wills to create, to repair, and to perfect. We may venture to go a little further and inquire whether we can really conceive a creative person being totally without concern when his creative intentions are not being fulfilled. In some ways it might be claimed that a creative will must include a will to bring to perfection whatever is failing to express its creative designs. I think we tend to believe that a genuine creator must wish to be a re-creator of what is damaged or imperfect. If we are thinking primarily of the will as re-creative I believe we shall be constrained to think that only the will as creative is equipped to fulfil the task of re-creation. The work of repairing and perfecting seems a natural task for the creative power which originally brought into existence the things which are failing to reach their intended perfection. An author is a natural authority upon his own work. We may be led to think that the creator of the world is the most perfect re-creator of the world. As creator we may say that he knows each being as an entity in itself and as one entity within the whole process of the natural world. His knowledge, as we may say, is both local and universal. Any re-creative agency other than the creator would be an intervening power whose will would not be naturally applicable to the created world. The intervention which was said to be saving would have an air of improvisation. It would have the appearance of an emergency operation or an impromptu mobilisation of such re-creative powers as happened to be available and applicable. All these rather glib descriptive phrases are never more than a short distance from collapsing into meaninglessness, but I believe that the total collapse never quite occurs. The gossamer threads are stretched to breaking point but they do not break.

We have the same sense of moving in a very rarefied atmosphere if we try to understand the situations in which a divine creative will may be impeded in the created world. If we think of entities in which there is no meaning in drawing a distinction between what they are and what they ought to be, it is difficult to think in what sense they may fail to be what they are intended to be. They are simply what they are as they are. If beings such as these impede the creative will of God, a re-creative act would consist in making new things which no longer impede the divine will simply in virtue of being what they are. The operation of the divine saving will would not be to bring the earlier set of things to perfection but to substitute for them another set of things. This is not an act of salvation but of rejection. I think in an obscure way we can see that a re-creative act of God is appropriate only to a personal being in which there is a meaningful distinction between what is the case and what ought to be. The whole mysterious being of such a being is not identical either with its actual state or with the state which it is intended to attain. We cannot contain its infinite being within the forms of thinking which are adapted to entities which are impersonal. Problems crowd upon us when we try to understand how the saving act of God may be done and, if we content ourselves with saying that the act in itself must always remain mysterious to us, we still face the very grave difficulty that no description of the act appears to be entirely free from moral objections. The problem remains of conceiving the saving act in a manner which does not reduce the autonomy of the moral agent. The dilemma is that an evil person cannot by an act of his evil will transform himself into a good person.

And if he is made good by a divine act of will, the transformation appears to override the autonomy of the moral agent. I know of no theory of divine grace which is not open to moral criticism. The Gospel always remains a mystery to the Law. At least, we may discard ways of thinking about the operation of grace which we can see to be inadequate. It is plain that grace cannot be adequately represented as a physical substance. If we think of it more in terms of personal influence, we are still thinking inadequately if we represent its operations as just like the influence of one finite will upon another. We know that God is not related to human beings exactly as they are related to one another. We should strive to eliminate problems about divine action that spring from the use of analogies which we know to be imperfect. Even so, I cannot persuade myself that the exclusion of linguistic muddles would leave no problem of divine grace. We may make some progress by thinking of the creative will of God as providing what we call the standards of personal being which are not external to personal being but standards which must be honoured by the beings which are entitled to be called personal. In true humility of spirit, which in fact we never attain, we may feel the subtle pressure of these standards which are at once creative and re-creative. Our moral autonomy is not annihilated but realised in responding to the intimations of our true being.

When the moral standard is interpreted as the creative and saving will of God it is plain that such a will is never exhaustively manifested in any of its particular expressions or manifestations. Its fullest revelation is in a personal being in whom there is no inconsistency between what is the case and what ought to be the case. There could be no complete revelation through the medium of the impersonal. And the revelation is always imperfect in personal lives where the incongruity between what is and what ought to be has not been overcome. It is the christian claim that in Christ we see the truth of our nature. His significance is not fully appreciated if he is treated as an external example which we must strive to emulate. As a perfect but particular embodiment of the creative and saving will of God he is active in all men, disposing them towards moral perfection and striving to re-create them when they turn away from the perfection to which they are called. The quest for moral perfection is far more than a quest for private excellence. It involves the attainment of right relationships with God and with our fellow-men. And it includes a right relation of re-created humanity to the natural world. The consummation is set in eternity, which lies far beyond the range of profitable description.

I have offered in these lectures some defence of the truth and excellence of christian theological ethics. I explained at the start that I was not giving a defence of christian theism or of the use of analogy in christian theology. My main concern was with the moral objections to theological ethics which sprang from a belief in the autonomy of the moral standard and in the autonomy of the moral agent. In order to prepare the way for a study of the theological interpretation of the moral standard as the creative and saving will of God, I spent several lectures in examining the nature and operation of physical and personal standards and in a study of some of the meanings of autonomy. In the later lectures, I sought to show that christian theological ethics rightly understood were not open to some of the more common moral objections and that they offered a reasonable interpretation of the whole of our moral experience while not ignoring or denying what is true in the claim that the moral standard and the moral agent are autonomous. I remain acutely conscious of all the inadequacies and confusions which are present in what I have written but I hope that I have said nothing which has encouraged enthusiasm on the one hand or superstition on the other. To that extent at least I may have fulfilled something of the intentions of the Reverend John Hulse in founding the lectureship which on this occasion I have had the honour of holding.

SHORT BIBLIOGRAPHY

MOORE, G. E. *Principia Ethica*. Cambridge University Press, 1903.

BROAD, C. D. *Five Types of Ethical Theory*. Kegan Paul, London, 1930.

TAYLOR, A. E. *Faith of a Moralist*. Macmillan, London, 1931.

OMAN, JOHN. *The Natural and the Supernatural*. Cambridge University Press, 1931.

BRUNNER, E. *The Divine Imperative*. Lutterworth, London, 1937.

McADOO, H. R. *Structure of Caroline Morality*. Longmans Green, London, 1949.

PRIOR, A. N. *Logic and the Basis of Ethics*. Oxford, Clarendon Press, 1949.

TOULMIN, S. *The Place of Reason in Ethics*. Cambridge University Press, 1950.

DODD, C. H. *Gospel and Law*. Cambridge University Press, 1951.

LEWIS, H. D. *Morals and Revelation*. Allen and Unwin, 1951.

THIELICKE, H. *Theologische Ethik*. J. C. B. Mohr, Tübingen, 1951, and later volumes.

HARE, R. M. *The Language of Morals*. Oxford, Clarendon Press, 1952.

NIEBUHR, H. R. *Christ and Culture*. Faber and Faber, London, 1952.

Readings in Ethical Theory, ed. W. Sellars and J. Hospers. New York, Appleton, Century, Cross, 1952.

BEACH, W. & NIEBUHR, H. R. *Christian Ethics*. Ronald, New York, 1955.

BONHOEFFER, D. *Ethics*, S.C.M., London, 1955.

THOMAS, G. F. *Christian Ethics and Moral Philosophy*. Charles Scribner's Sons, New York, 1955.

NOWELL-SMITH, P. H. *Ethics*. Pelican reprint, 1956.

BARTH, KARL. *Church Dogmatics*. Volume II, Part 2. *Doctrine of God*. T. and T. Clark, Edinburgh, 1957.

Faith and ethics: The Theology of H. R. Niebuhr, ed. P. Ramsey. Harper, New York, 1957.

LACK, D. *Evolutionary Theory and Christian Belief*. The unresolved conflict. Methuen, London, 1957.

MACKINNON, D. M. *A Study in Ethical Theory*. A. and C. Black. London, 1957.

Faith and Logic, ed. B. Mitchell. Allen and Unwin, London, 1957.

HEPBURN, R. W. *Christianity and Paradox. Critical studies in Twentieth Century Theology*. Watts, London, 1958.

GILLEMAN GÉRARD. *The Primacy of Charity in Moral Theology*. Burns and Oates, London, 1959.

MASCALL, E. L. *The Importance of Being Human*. Some aspects of the christian doctrine of man. Oxford University Press, 1959.

MANSON, T. W. *Ethics and the Gospel*. S.C.M., London, 1960.

MACLAGAN, W. G. *The Theological Frontier of Ethics*. Allen and Unwin, London, 1961.

Prospect for Metaphysics, ed. I. T. Ramsey. Allen and Unwin, London, 1961.

KNOX, JOHN. *The Ethic of Jesus in the Teaching of the Church*. Epworth, London, 1962.

Soundings. Essays concerning christian understanding. Ed. A. R. Vidler. Cambridge University Press, 1962.

LEHMANN, P. L. *Ethics in a Christian Context*. S.C.M., London, 1963.

TILLICH, PAUL. *Morality and Beyond*. Routledge and Kegan Paul, London, 1964.

WADDAMS, H. *A new Introduction to Moral Theology*. S.C.M., London, 1964.

INDEX

INDEX